EVERYDAY MATTERS

MATTERS

Intersections of Life and Faith

L. Gregory Jones

ABINGDON PRESS / Nashville

EVERYDAY MATTERS
INTERSECTIONS OF LIFE AND FAITH

This book is printed on acid-free, elemental-chlorine–free paper.

Library of Congress Cataloging-in-Publication Data

Jones, L. Gregory.
  Everyday matters : intersections of life and faith / L. Gregory Jones.

    p. cm.
  ISBN 0-687-07528-9 (pbk. : alk. paper)
  1. Christian life--Meditations. I. Title.
  BV4501.3.J656 2003
  248.4--dc21

                                                        2003012544

Scripture quotations, unless otherwise noted, are from the New Revised Standard Version of the Bible, copyright © 1989, by the Division of Christian Education of the National Council of the Churches of Christ in the United States of America. Used by permission.

These articles first appeared in the *Christian Century.* Copyright 1997, 1998, 1999, 2000, 2001, 2002 Christian Century foundation. Reprinted by permission.

03 04 05 06 07 08 09 10 11 12 — 10 9 8 7 6 5 4 3 2 1

MANUFACTURED IN THE UNITED STATES OF AMERICA

For

Nathan Jameson
Benjamin Alexander
Sarah Pendleton

with love, gratitude, and hope

CONTENTS

PREFACE

WE LONG TO FIND a center for our lives that helps us hold things together, make connections, and find networks of meaning and purpose that enable us to flourish. Christians believe such a center is found in God's love for us made manifest in Jesus Christ. We are drawn to Christ as the One who weaves together the fragmented parts of our own lives, and who reconnects us to God and to one another. This is a daunting claim, and yet in our worship we testify to Christ's significance as the One in whom the whole world was made and who loves each of us in our particularity.

Yet we live in a world marked by fragmentation and brokenness, a world where it is often difficult to make connections, much less to sustain them. Sometimes this fragmentation is explicitly encouraged—we are taught to keep religion separate from politics, to separate our private commitments from our public understandings. At other times this fragmentation is implicitly assumed—we simply move through different arenas of our lives as if they are not connected to each other. But the results are the same: Rather than cultivating coherence, we find ourselves beset by fragments.

This is intensified by the brokenness of our lives and of the world in which we live. Christians identify this as the effects of sin. We are haunted by the legacies and memories of destructiveness that are social as well as intensely personal. We long for the healing and wholeness that we believe can come only through forgiveness, a redeeming of the past for the sake of a new future.

How might we address this brokenness and fragmentation in faithful, life-giving ways? How might we explore ways of addressing our longing for a center that holds, a center that will help us make the connections that provide a sense of wholeness?

That is the task of the gospel in any age, but it has particular importance in our time. We need to connect our faith in Christ with the everyday issues that we think about, struggle with, and hope for in our lives and our world.

Early in 1997, the editors of *The Christian Century*, a significant Christian periodical, initiated a new column that would address such issues. They entitled the column "Faith Matters," and they asked me to serve as one of four regular contributors to the column. I happily agreed and began a practice that has been as enjoyable as it has been challenging.

The practice is to write a 1,000-word reflection that brings the resources of Christian faith to bear on important questions, issues, or struggles of people's lives. The challenge is to be substantive without rambling, to offer insights and questions without being superficial.

Over the years that I have written these columns, I have found that the feared deadlines have diminished in significance as this practice has helped reshape the connections I make in my own thinking and living. I had wondered whether I could keep finding different topics to address, or if I could stay fresh, to keep the pace of a regular column. But I have discovered that in everyday life there are important issues and significant opportunities to reflect on the intersections of life and Christian faith.

This book offers a selection of my columns over a five-year period, from 1997 to 2002, with the date(s) on which each originally appeared in *The Christian Century*. As columns have appeared, I have recurrently been asked by laity and clergy alike if there might be a setting or settings to discuss the issues I raise. I am encouraged by such interest, for the intersections of life and faith call for faithful discernment with other people. Indeed, as you will see from the structure of the book, these reflections call for communities of friends and mentors to engage in ongoing discernment about how to learn, how to be formed and transformed, in ways that sustain life-giving virtues. This includes grappling with difficult challenges along the path of our journey. I believe that Christian life, lived at its best, calls for this commitment to a journey that does not shy away from challenges. Rather, we are sustained by our ongoing life of learning in the company of friends and mentors.

In order to facilitate conversation, I have added questions for further reflection and discussion following each chapter. I hope that readers will find friends, study groups, or classes with which to continue to engage these issues in relation to God and the complexities of the world, and of our lives.

I have been blessed by a rich company of friends and colleagues in this journey who have shaped this book. I am grateful to David Heim and Debra Bendis at *The Christian Century,* both for their original invitation and for their support, their patience, and their careful editing over the years. I am thankful for the efforts of my assistants, especially Mary Ann Andrus and Amy Turnbull, who remind me of deadlines and aid my efforts in so many ways. And I am particularly grateful to Stephan Turnbull, a doctoral student in New Testament at Duke, who worked thoughtfully and patiently in developing a structure for the book and in drafting the questions.

My friend and colleague Kevin Armstrong believed in the potential significance of this project, and he helped me to see the ways in which it might be of service to folks interested in making connections between their faith and their everyday lives. I am thankful for his suggestions and his careful reading of the questions and the columns. Even more, I am thankful for the ways in which our friendship over the years has helped shape the vision I articulate in these pages.

In addition, there are countless colleagues and friends, especially among the faculty, students, and staff at Duke Divinity School, who have graciously talked through themes and issues with me in ways that have enhanced the quality of my own thinking. Teaching and serving with my colleagues at Duke is a blessing and a privilege.

Most of all, I want to thank my family. My wife, Susan, who is my partner in ministry and life, is the one who first envisioned this book. She has steadfastly guided me in both the composition of the original columns and in shaping the contours of the book. More generally, she has shaped the person I am in more ways than I can imagine and certainly with more graciousness than I deserve. She is also my best critic and most faithful source of encouragement. Words are inadequate to express my gratitude for her love, her friendship, and her ministry.

Susan has also helped me to become a better parent as we, by God's grace, have engaged the joys and travails of rearing our three wonderful children, Nathan, Ben, and Sarah. The kids have been remarkably patient with a father who has had his own growing up to do and one who has often had to excuse himself at odd times in order to write "one of those columns." They are also a source of unending joy and blessing. They appear from time to time in these pages, always with their permission. They appear because my everyday life is so shaped by them, because they often ask poignant questions and offer key insights, and because some of our most important intersections of life and faith these days have to do with struggles about what it means to rear children faithfully and to rear faithful children. This book is dedicated to them, with a sense of gratitude, joy, and hope that their future will be marked by a sense of God's presence in everyday matters, and that they will grow in the Christian faith knowing that every day matters.

PART 1

BECOMING CHRISTIANS

1

ONE THAT MATTERS

WE WERE driving home from soccer practice. I was talking with my 11-year-old son about his team and the drills they had done that evening. I did not anticipate the turn our conversation was about to take.

"What does a divinity school do, anyway?" he asked. Some weeks earlier he had asked me what a "dean" was. I had suggested that a dean was analogous to the principal of his elementary school. He had been content with that and did not raise any further questions.

I told him that a divinity school is a place where people go to learn how to become ministers. I mentioned the names of some ministers he knew, then added: "They came to divinity school so they could study the Bible, learn to preach and lead worship, and develop the skills necessary to be ministers of a congregation."

"Oh," he replied. I thought this had settled the matter. But then he spoke again. "Dad," he asked, "don't you think a divinity school ought to spend more time learning about God?"

I didn't quite know what to say. After all, he was exactly right. My description of a divinity school had inadvertently left out the One who ought to be the central focus of the school's activities. That was ironic, since I have spent much of the last year thinking about how and why a Christian divinity school needs to link together the love of learning and the desire for God. Yet my son noticed that my description listed activities of the ministry that could in principle be conducted without reference to God.

How much of church and seminary life is conducted as if God does not really matter? When we initiate new Christians into the faith, do we teach them to diagnose and renounce false ideas about God so that they and we are more likely to worship God faithfully? Archbishop William Temple's warning ought to haunt us: "If you have a false idea of God, the more religious you are, the worse it is for you—it were better for you to be an atheist."

We have for so long assumed that "everyone" knows what we are talking about when we refer to God that we have not tested the adequacy of our understanding or the faithfulness of our worship. Too often the language has lost its force, because we are unclear whom we are addressing or about whom we are critically reflecting. Further, we are increasingly discovering that people are referring to God in diverse and often incompatible ways—even among Christians, not to mention among those who adhere to diverse religious traditions.

Have we adequately helped one another learn what it means to address God faithfully in prayer or worship? Or to identify who Christians believe God is and how God is related to the world and to our lives? To be sure, focusing on God in these ways will lead us into difficult debates and issues of discernment. Yet too often we have avoided testing our own judgments about a basic question: How do we identify God and understand God's relationship to the world and my life?

A few years ago, I asked a gathering of church folks—a group that represented a wide diversity of Christian traditions, from evangelical to mainline Protestant to Roman Catholic—how they would characterize the Christian understanding of God to someone who knows absolutely nothing of the Christian faith. There was a long silence. Finally, one person volunteered a suggestion. He said, "God is a force that has created things."

I asked for ways to enrich, modify or rework this phrase. There were no takers. So I asked a specific question: "Some things? All things?" The original person, worried by my suggestion, favored a cautious approach. "Some things."

There we had it: "God is a force that has created some things." This seemed acceptable, until I asked whether people would be willing to begin a prayer addressed to God in this way. They didn't think so, but were puzzled about where to move from there.

I suspect that we might have made more progress had I begun by asking people to reflect on the ways they address God in prayer. After all, St. Gregory of Sinai suggested that Christian prayer entails "sharing in the divine nature." He even claimed that "prayer is God."

In Christian prayer we learn to develop a relationship with the One to whom we pray. Such a relationship is crucial, for it helps us deepen our understanding of God and renounce the ways in which we have constructed "god" in our own image. Similarly, it is only through developing a relationship with someone that I slowly learn how to describe his or her character. Reading about a person is no substitute for getting to know her. Developing a relationship with God involves both learning how to pray and learning more about the One to whom we pray.

The disciples asked Jesus, "Lord, teach us to pray." In such prayer the disciples discovered communion with God, the One whom Jesus addressed as "Abba." They also discovered that prayer and the knowledge and love of God are closely related. That is why the Eastern Christian tradition has always emphasized the close relationship between prayer and theology. As one maxim puts it, "The person who prays is a true theologian and the true theologian is one who prays."

Perhaps it was my son's own yearning to understand more

about the God whom we worship that led him to ask his follow-up question. Or maybe it was a sense that, for all of our involvement in church activities, he—like the disciples—wants to learn better how to pray. Whatever the reason, his question reminds us that the deepest issue is not what we do at school, or in our vocation, but how we connect our learning and our living to a desire to know and love the God of Jesus Christ.

May 20–27, 1998

Reflection / Discussion Questions

1. The phrases "God Bless America," "One Nation Under God," and "In God We Trust" have become commonplace—and controversial—in American culture. When are those phrases used, and how are they interpreted differently by different people?
2. A bumper sticker reads, "If you're living like there is no God, you'd better be right." Would your way of life change significantly if you could suddenly know for sure that there really was no God? Would it change if you were more aware of the presence of God in your life? And if so, in what ways?
3. Write a few sentences describing your understanding of God. Discuss them with other Christians or with your pastor. Does your understanding of God encourage or hinder prayer? How does it shape the way that you pray?
4. Belief in the existence of God is not the same thing as living one's life as a worshiper of God. James 2:19 says, "You believe that God is one; you do well. Even the demons believe—and shudder." What was James trying to encourage among the Christians to whom he wrote?

16

2

GOD'S HOLINESS

THE RABBI PUT the question to my friend directly: "Do Christians believe that God is holy?" My friend was initially taken aback; she thought of the popularity of the hymn "Holy, Holy, Holy," and of her love of passages in Exodus, Isaiah and Revelation that emphasize the holiness of God. She recalled the passage in the Lord's Prayer where we indicate that God's name is hallowed. "What is the rabbi really asking?" she wondered to herself.

The rabbi continued, "When I ask Jews to identify one word that comes to mind when they think of God, they typically answer 'holy.' But when I ask Christians, the consistent answer is 'love.' So I began to wonder, what do Christians think about God's holiness?"

My friend got to thinking about whether contemporary Christians have an appropriate sense of the holiness of God. She asked me whether I, as a United Methodist, thought that heirs of the Wesleyan tradition emphasized God's holiness more than other traditions did. A bit chagrined, I replied that I thought most United Methodists would refer to God as love, as friend or parent, or even as judge, before referring to God as holy.

Why this aversion to referring to God's holiness? Does it affect the way we understand God, worship God, pray to God? Often we appeal to God as love, friend or parent as a way of emphasizing God's approachability and desire for relationship with us. The God of Jesus Christ, we stress to ourselves and others, is not a cold, impersonal deity far removed from the concerns of humanity.

Furthermore, we emphasize God's love as a counter-balance to images that many people have of an excessively austere, judging, wrathful God. We want to know that God ultimately loves us, redeems us, forgives us; we want to know that mercy does indeed triumph over judgment.

But in the process, have we domesticated God? Have we lost sight of God's majestic holiness? Has our emphasis on God's love turned too much attention to our subjectivity in prayer, rather than to the hallowed character of God's name? In his classic book, *Beginning to Pray,* Anthony Bloom begins by asking us to reflect on what it means to desire to be in God's presence: "When we read the gospel and the image of Christ becomes compelling, glorious, when we pray and we become aware of the greatness, the holiness of God, do we ever say, 'I am unworthy that he should come near me'? Not to speak of all the occasions when we should be aware that he cannot come to us because we are not there to receive him. We want something *from* him, not *him* at all. Is that a relationship?"

To be sure, there are distorted conceptions of human unworthiness that have wreaked havoc in congregations and in lives. Such conceptions have been grounded in views of God's judgment and wrath that have typically ignored God's mercy and love. But perhaps the pendulum has swung too far in the opposite direction. Too often we proclaim, at least implicitly if not explicitly, an always accessible, nice God who has few if any standards.

Bloom's point is that if we want to be in genuine relationship with God, we need to ponder more fully God's character—including God's holiness. God should not be simply the unknown object of sentimental devotion, or the one who endorses insatiable human desires. Rather, we should get to

know and love the God who has been revealed to humanity—in fear of God's holiness, as well as in profound gratitude for God's extravagant mercy.

This suggests that we need to prepare ourselves for
prayer; we need to prepare ourselves for relationship with
the God whose forgiveness makes it possible for us to turn
to God.

Bloom notes:

> What we must start with, if we wish to pray, is the certainty
> that we are sinners in need of salvation, that we are cut off
> from God and that we cannot live without him and that all
> we can offer God is our desperate longing to be made such
> that God will receive us, receive us in repentance, receive us
> with mercy and with love. And so, from the outset, prayer is
> really our humble ascent towards God, a moment when we
> turn Godwards, shy of coming near, knowing that if we meet
> him too soon, before his grace has had time to help us to be
> capable of meeting him, it will be judgment. And all we can
> do is to turn to him with all the reverence, all the veneration,
> the worshipful adoration, the fear of God of which we are
> capable, with all the attention and earnestness which we may
> possess, and ask him to do something with us that will make
> us capable of meeting him face to face, not for judgment, nor
> for condemnation, but for eternal life.

We can only understand and faithfully live in relationship
to God's holiness if we prepare ourselves to receive God's
extravagant mercy. Perhaps our unwillingness to think about
God in terms of holiness is because we have so trivialized
and sentimentalized our understandings of what it means to
think of God in terms of love, friendship or forgiveness.
After all, authentically Christian versions of love, friendship
and forgiveness are all closely linked with a call to become
holy.

Could it be that the rabbi rather innocently exposed a
weakness in contemporary Christianity's understanding and
worship of God? We must include God's holiness in our

identification of God's love if we are to faithfully address the God of Exodus, Isaiah and Revelation.

October 20, 1999

Reflection / Discussion Questions

1. What does it mean to say that God is holy? Read Exodus 3:1-17; Isaiah 6:1-13; and Revelation 4:1–5:14 to help you form a biblical answer.
2. How do you feel about the phrase "the fear of God"? Does it conjure up unbalanced fright and terror or does it connote reverential worship and healthy awe? Explain.
3. The apostle Paul often refers to Christians as saints or "holy ones." We are holy because Jesus Christ has made us so. As a "holy one," what can you do to make the ways and habits of your life more holy?

3

SWIMMING IN THE DEEP END

THE PRINCIPAL of the Catholic high school was taken aback by the phone call. It came from an inmate in a nearby prison. He was known to be wealthy, but had been incarcerated for having acquired some of his wealth by fradulent means. Now the man was offering to make a significant donation to the school.

In return for this donation, the inmate wanted the high school to make it possible for his adult son, a high school dropout, to receive a high school diploma. As the principal inquired further, it became apparent that the inmate did not want the son to have to do anything to earn the diploma. He simply wanted the son to be sent a diploma.

The principal was flabbergasted. Why, she asked the inmate, did he care so much that his son, now in business for himself, received his diploma? "Because education is important," replied the inmate.

The reply is humorous, but at the same time tragic, because it was spoken in utter seriousness. It points to a cultural crisis: people believe and continue to assert that education is important, but the assertion is increasingly disconnected from the ends at which education aims or the process by which students learn to care about those ends.

Why is education important? Is it simply a formal certification that acknowledges having made it through a certain number of years of school? A way of designating that people have done their time?

Or perhaps, less pejoratively but no less problematically, education is important only as a means of certifying that people have some basic skills necessary for minimal job performance. While such certification is important to a community's ability to function, it does not foster communities of people who care about teaching and function, it does not foster communities of people who care about teaching and learning— nor is it likely to produce the next generation's teachers.

I believe that education is important because human flourishing requires that we undertake a lifelong process of formation, of seeking to understand and master a variety of modes of inquiry. Only through a patient, often painful process of learning disciplines do we begin to cultivate the character, shape the habits, acquire the virtues and discern the truth that students and teachers alike need.

Education is important not only in its formal settings, but also—and more determinatively—in its lifelong commitments. Diplomas and degrees are not the aim of education so much as they are markers of achievement on a longer and richer journey.

If the ends of education can be discovered only through a lifelong journey, then perhaps we need to focus less on the markers—standardized tests, diplomas and degrees—and more on the ways we shape one another's habits through our practices of education in schools and congregations. Perhaps we need richer conceptions of formation to accompany our convictions about education.

We seem to understand the importance of education only retrospectively, as the fruit of habits learned over a lifetime. Initially, we learn how to do things by means extrinsic to us. We learn to spell, to add or to say the Lord's Prayer by repeating the words, numbers or phrases that others teach us. Similarly, we learn to play the scales of a piano by having another show us how to move our hands.

Over time, we transform those extrinsic modes of learning into intrinsic habits. We begin to understand the ways in which the alphabet is used to create words, and grammar to construct sentences. We learn how the dynamics of addition and subtraction are linked to multiplication and division, and eventually to theorems of algebra. We begin to discover how the Lord's Prayer shapes a relationship with God and an understanding of God that invite other patterns of prayer and worship. We master the rhythm of the scales and begin to explore the chords and patterns of beautiful music.

Eventually these modes of practice and inquiry become a part of our lives. We then continue to learn by making new connections between practices, between disciplines, between modes of inquiry. Over time we become equipped to advance our understanding even further by criticizing poor theories, challenging false constructions, correcting distorted practices and seeing possibilities that others have not seen.

Our education proceeds toward increasingly intrinsic patterns of inquiry, practice and discipline. We discover that our ends are being transformed and our understanding of the truth is being deepened through our lifelong commitment to learning. There are no shortcuts, whether in our mastery of language, our understanding of mathematics, our knowledge and love of God, or our musical theory and practice.

Anglican theologian W. H. Vanstone once observed that the church is like a swimming pool in which all the noise comes from the shallow end. Most of the wisdom is to be found in the deep end, among those who have taken the time, and cultivated the habits and disciplines, to learn to swim in deeper waters. Vanstone was particularly concerned about the shallow spirituality in the churches, but his comments are also true of our knowledge and our love of God, of the world and of the disciplines we seek to understand and practice. If we are to love God with all of our mind as well as our heart, soul and strength, then we need the kind of sustained learning that leads us into the deep end of the pool.

Unfortunately in our culture—inside and outside the churches—too much of the noise is coming from the shallow end. We laugh at a wealthy man trying to buy his son a degree, but how different is he from our own attitudes and actual practices about education? Do we care more about the degrees or the certification than the habits of learning? Do we really want to understand, to live, the importance of education?

July 5–12, 2000

Reflection / Discussion Questions

1. What comes to your mind when you hear the word *education*? Do you think of school, or life experience, or both? What do we mean when we say that something we have experienced "was a real education"?
2. Proverbs 8:10-11 says, "Take my instruction instead of silver, / and knowledge rather than choice gold; / for wisdom is better than jewels, / and all that you may desire cannot compare with her." Why does the Bible teach that these virtues have a higher value than great wealth? Do you spend more energy pursuing knowledge and wisdom or "gold" and "jewels"?
3. Do you believe that education is important for a church or for society? Explain your answer. What can you do in your community to value the process of education? What are other Christian communities in your area doing to foster education?
4. Education is a lifelong process, and we never outgrow our role as a learner. What opportunities might you take advantage of, or what attitudes might you change that will help you continue to learn and grow?

4

WHY BOTHER TO THINK?

ONE OF THE central characters in Berke Breathed's wonderful comic strip *Bloom County* was a penguin named Opus. One day Opus decided he wanted to give up television and become more learned. As he walked up the steps of the "Publik Library," Opus announced: "Attention, dark world of electronic gratification. . . . I would like to announce my intellectualization! No more tv! No boob tube-a-roo! 'Twas turning my noodle to video goo! Yes, there's something much better for smart chaps like me. . . . From what I have heard, it's known as 'to read'! Books! I'll read books! Be they large or quite dinky! Straight from the shelves all musty and stinky! Faulkner! O'Neill! Twain and Saul Bellow! . . . I think I'll curl up with a few of those fellows! Yes, I'll soon be well-read! Such a fab thing to be! I've allowed plenty of time, at least an hour . . . or three."

Opus then stands bewildered in the midst of shelves of books that climb to the sky. The shelves appear to be closing in around him. In the last frame, Opus is back home, munching on a snack, in front of the television, as a voice from the television calls out, "Gilligan!" (*Bloom County Babylon*).

Many of us share Opus's experience. We begin with an enthusiasm for learning and thinking, but when confronted with the sheer magnitude of how much there is to learn, how demanding it is to think, we are tempted to revert back to the mind-numbing impact of *Gilligan's Island*. Then we face anew the question, "Why bother to think?"

One could offer a variety of plausible answers: the unthinking life is not worth living; the health of democracy depends on citizens' thoughtful engagement; we cannot really avoid thinking, so we might as well do it well; we want to try to make sense of the world and of our lives, and understand how our convictions hold together; we need to be equipped to challenge false ideologies, partial truths, and deceptions of ourselves and others.

All of these are worthy reasons, yet none of them may be sufficient to overcome the inertia cultivated by long habits of passivity and superficial reflection. I believe that Chaim Potok offers a particularly compelling answer. In his novel *In the Beginning,* Potok writes: "A shallow mind is a sin against God."

Why is a shallow mind a sin? In part, because both Jews and Christians have been commanded "to love the Lord your God with all of your heart, soul, mind and strength." You cannot love God with all of your mind and leave it untended. As creatures created in the image and likeness of God, we are called to think, motivated by a desire to know and love God truthfully and faithfully.

We are called to think constructively, to make sense of the world around us, our own lives and our understanding of God. Our thinking is shaped by many of the questions that three- and four-year-olds typically ask: Is there a God? Where does God live? Why do people die? Is there hope for people after they die? Why are there people who do bad things? Why do friends do mean things to me?

Contrary to the presumptions of many skeptical academics, there are powerful and compelling responses to these questions. These responses have been shaped by the rich resources of our forebears, including such intellectual giants as St. Augustine and St. Thomas Aquinas. They also require contemporary reformulation and reflection.

There are too many "religious" people who become religious precisely to avoid having to think. They simply want to accept everything "on faith." They fall prey to the problem evident in the children's sermon in which a pastor asked the kids, "What I am thinking of is brown, has a bushy tail, and gathers acorns every fall." After a brief silence, a little boy raises his hand and says, "I am sure the right answer is Jesus, but it sure sounds like a squirrel to me."

Unthinking religious people are sure the right answer is "Jesus" (or an equivalent), even before any questions have been asked. Such unthinking religiosity lapses into traditionalism, which Jaroslav Pelikan calls "the dead faith of the living." By contrast, we need the vitality of thinking in connection to tradition, which Pelikan calls "the living faith of the dead." Traditionalism may be tempted to ignore the importance of thinking, but vital traditions require careful thought precisely so that we can remember the past well for the sake of the future.

Further, we need to think to deepen our minds, in order to challenge and criticize our false gods and other sins. That is, we need to think in order to unlearn bad habits that have shaped and continue to shape our lives—such habits as cynicism, fatalism, narcissism or prejudice. Thinking leaves us open to correction and growth, to continuing to see our horizons expanded and our lives transformed.

Ultimately, we ought to bother to think because our fidelity to God, and our human flourishing, require it. We need to learn how to think well, which involves both constructive and critical moments. We should not be overwhelmed by what we do not know, but appreciate what we can know as we cultivate a love of learning and a desire for God. After all, there are only so many episodes of *Gilligan* to watch.

November 15, 2000

Reflection / Discussion Questions

1. How many hours do you spend every day wherein your primary activity is watching television? How many hours do you spend on the primary activity of thinking? Reflect on / discuss how your particular use of time impacts your life and the lives of those around you.

2. Are there any political or ethical questions about which you would like to spend more time thinking or reading and learning? Reflect on these questions, discuss them with others, and find resources you can read about them to help you be more informed.

3. Potok wrote, "A shallow mind is a sin against God." Read Deuteronomy 6:5; Mark 12:29-30; and Luke 10:27. What does it mean to love the Lord with all of your mind? To what does your mind wander when it is unoccupied? How can you use your mind to cultivate a love for God and to serve your neighbor?

5

PUTTING ON NEW CLOTHES

Hans CHRISTIAN ANDERSEN tells about an emperor who was so fond of new clothes that he spent all his money on them. Alas, the emperor was so committed to his clothes that he neglected to take care of his people's needs. Instead, he spent all his time in his dressing room, admiring his garments.

One day two swindlers came and claimed they were weavers who could weave the "finest cloth imaginable." Their colors and patterns, they said, were exceptionally beautiful, and the clothes possessed a wonderful quality— they were invisible to any man who was unfit for his office, or who was hopelessly stupid.

The emperor was impressed at the prospect of finding out which people in the empire were unfit for their posts, as well as telling the clever from the stupid. So he gave the men large amounts of money. The men pocketed the money and pretended to be weaving cloth.

Eventually, the emperor became curious about the progress on the clothes and decided to send his "honest old minister" to the weavers. The emperor was sure that the minister's unquestionable intelligence and fitness for office would make him a good emissary. But the minister could not see the cloth. He began to question his own intelligence and fitness for office and decided not to tell anyone that he had been unable to see the material.

Instead, he announced that the cloth "is very pretty—quite enchanting! . . . What a pattern, and what colors! I shall tell the emperor that I am very much pleased with it." Eventually the emperor himself went to see how the clothes were coming. What a shock when he realized that he saw nothing at all! But he did not want to admit that he was stupid or unfit to be emperor, so he announced that the cloth was very beautiful, and all the courtiers rapidly agreed.

The next day, the emperor took part in a great procession, and everyone pretended that they saw his new clothes. No one wanted to be shown to be unfit for his office or too stupid. But then a child spoke up.

"But he has nothing on at all," the child said. The people whispered to each other. "The child said he has nothing on!" "He has nothing on at all!" cried all the people at last. And the emperor too was worried, for it seemed to him that they were right. But he thought to himself, "I must go through with the procession." And he continued in the procession, wearing nothing at all.

Another great storyteller, Jesus of Nazareth, said, "Except as you become a little child. . . ." It was, after all, a child who was the only one with the courage to speak the truth about the emperor's (lack of) new clothes. Except for the witness of that child, everyone in the city was willing to live in a world of deception and lies. Everyone was captured by fear—fear of the powerful, fear caused by the grip of sin. Even after the child names the truth, the people and the emperor do not have the resources to know how to change their way of life. And so the emperor continues with the charade.

The emperor's new clothes allowed him, and others around him, to pretend to see something that wasn't there. By contrast, the clothes that Christians put on in baptism (see Galatians 3:27) invite us, and others around us, to see that which really is there—to become truthful with ourselves and one another in fidelity to God.

But what happens when we clothe ourselves with Christ? Does the transformation occur overnight, as if by some magic wand? Or does it begin a process of being initiated into habits and practices of a way of life, an initiation in which we become apprentices to those who have gone before us?

In the early church, entry into the Christian community was marked by an apprenticeship guided by sponsors. At the time of baptism on Easter, new Christians signified the power of their turning from a world of sin and deception to a life clothed in Christ. Unlike the emperor's new clothes, the apprentice's new clothes were a sign of commitment to see what really *is* there in the world—in praise and penitence.

Jesus' announcement and enactment of God's inbreaking reign calls disciples then and now into a new community marked by forgiveness and repentance. In so doing, God is shaping a truthful community capable of radical discipleship and witness in the world.

The story of the emperor's new clothes reminds us that the issue we face is not whether we will be apprentices or not. We are apprentices who are influenced by others, for good or for ill. In the world of the emperor, we are shaped by sin and deception. Whether we are swindlers who deceive others for the sake of our own gain, or townspeople so concerned about appearances that we are unwilling and even unable to discern the truth, we become chained to habits of sin and being sinned against. Our lives become marked by fear.

The real issue is whether we are willing to don the apprentice's new clothes and to struggle to bear witness with one another to the truthful and life-giving character of God's inbreaking reign. In so doing, we learn to "be not afraid" as we find a sense of new life. But that will also require that we recover the importance of shaping our own and one another's lives in habits and practices that enable us to unlearn the world of emperors and to learn to see the world as apprentices to the true Master.

March 10, 1999

Reflection / Discussion Questions

1. Imagine that you are a child in the midst of your own current life. Try to imagine the simple and telling questions that you would ask of yourself and those around you.
2. Galatians 3:27 associates our new clothes with our baptism, the birthplace of who we are in Christ. What "clothes" do you wear that reflect your identity as a Christian? What clothes should you change?
3. Baptism as described in Galatians 3:27 and in the historic practice of the Christian church is at least as much about community as it is about individuals. The words for "you" in this passage, for example, are all plural. What "clothes" does your congregation wear as a result of and as a witness to its Christian identity?
4. The second half of the reading suggests that apprenticeship and community are valuable assets for developing character. How does your congregation foster such relationships and assets for character development?

6

MUNDANE EXCELLENCE

THE MAJOR DIFFERENCE between swimmers who win Olympic medals and those who don't is not talent, but the care and consistency with which Olympic swimmers engage in the mundane activities that prepare them for competition. This is the conclusion of sociologist Daniel F. Chambliss in his essay "The Mundanity of Excellence," a report on a three-year empirical study of excellent swimmers.

To be sure, there are natural differences in ability that we typically identify as talent. But Chambliss believes that when we see the full flowering of someone's careful practices, we attribute that achievement to "talent" because we are not remembering the years of practice and the cultivation of habits and techniques that come together to constitute excellence. "Of course there is no secret; there is only the doing of all those little things, each one done correctly, time and again, until excellence in every detail becomes a firmly ingrained habit, an ordinary part of one's everyday life."

We learn from other excellent athletes, performers and artists about the centrality of this attention to detail, habit and the doing of "ordinary things" day by day. This is as true of Michael Jordan as of Isaac Stern, of Cal Ripken as of Dorothy Hamill. Whether it was shooting endless free throws or practicing scales, taking ground balls or focusing on school figures, their excellence was shaped by disciplined attention to the little things.

Yet this is one of the most difficult things to teach to beginners wanting to become athletes, musicians or artists. I coach a basketball team of 9–11-year-old boys. They never want to practice—they want to scrimmage so they can show off their three-pointers or their spectacular "Michael Jordan moves." It is difficult to help them understand Jordan's commitment to the mundane tasks of repetition, discipline and practice.

Obviously, some kids on the team have more athletic ability than others. But I am also acutely aware that some of the kids with a lot of natural ability won't ever develop that ability, whereas some others, those who put in the effort, will likely do much better over time.

Commitment to the little things is crucial to the religious life as well. We do not often think in those terms. We are more likely to focus on the importance of dramatic conversions, overwhelming encounters with God, and powerful moments of prayer. We search for peak experiences and fear that some people have a talent for the religious life, a talent that we are somehow missing.

Kathleen Norris writes in *The Quotidian Mysteries*: "In our life of faith . . . as well as in our most intimate relationships with other people, our task is to transform the high romance of conversion, the fervor of a religious call, into daily commitment. Into the sort of friendship that transcends infatuation and can endure all things. Our desire is to love God and each other, in stable relationships that, like any good marriage, remain open to surprises and receptive to grace."

Might our receptivity to grace be shaped by our commitment to the mundane? We are enjoined to pray for our "daily" bread and told not to be anxious for tomorrow. Could it be that Christian life is marked by tending to the daily activities of worship, work, study and community—and that these activities, when taken together, comprise faithfulness to God? As Norris writes a few pages later, "It is a paradox of human life that in worship, as in human love, it is in the routine and the everyday that we find the possibilities for the greatest transformation."

What if our conceptions of Christian life were to return to the importance of mundane activities that are "done correctly, time and again, until excellence in every detail becomes a firmly ingrained habit, an ordinary part of one's everyday life"? This would include the quality of loving care and attention for such daily, routine tasks as praying the Psalms and doing the laundry, offering signs of mercy as well as justice, caring for others and carefully studying texts.

We tend to nod knowingly as if of course we know that these things are important. But notice how little we tend to emphasize these things for "beginners" who want to learn about Christian faith and life. I have seen and participated in too many "new member" classes or confirmation programs in which the message communicated is that Christian life doesn't ask too much. We tend to communicate through our initiation practices that Christian life is more about "scrimmaging" than it is about engaging in daily routines, disciplines and practices that open us to God's grace.

Pondering the mundanity of excellence might return us to emphasizing those ordinary disciplines, those "school figures" that are conducive to shaping a faithful Christian life. The early Christians thought these included basic activities of hospitality and reconciliation, as well as learning to pray the Lord's Prayer and to recite the Apostles' Creed (as well as understanding why they are important). Over the centuries, others have added catechisms, the sacraments, means of grace or other particular basic themes.

This emphasis might enable us to recognize that the major difference between many of the saintly figures of the church and us is not their "natural talent" or disposition. Rather, it is the way their habits, disciplines and practices prepared them, in gracious openness to God's work, to live extraordinarily faithful lives.

January 2–9, 2002

Reflection / Discussion Questions

1. What routines in your life happen so regularly that you could call them habits? Have you created these habits intentionally or have they arisen unnoticed in the course of daily living?

2. "First you make your habits, then your habits make you." This old proverb reveals a sobering truth. What habits of behavior and thought shape your character? Would you like to quit some old practices and start some new ones? Established patterns are difficult to change, but habits can be formed one day at a time.

3. In Deuteronomy 6:4-9, God tells the Israelites how to shape themselves and their memories around habitual recall of God's commandments. What are the habits of your spiritual life? Prayer? Bible study? Acts of charity and Christian obedience? Are there some habits you will make plans to change? What can you learn from the regularity of the instruction in Deuteronomy 6?

7

GRACE-FULL GESTURES

IN HIS WONDERFUL MEMOIR *Open Secrets,* Richard Lischer describes a personal conflict that developed between Lischer and Leonard, a lay leader in the congregation. Their conflict had the potential to erupt into a major split in the congregation. But each man remained committed to the ministry of the church. When a woman who lived near Leonard overdosed on pills, Lischer forgot that he wasn't on speaking terms with his parishioner and called to ask Leonard to accompany him to the woman's house.

Their shared ministry in this setting provided an opportunity for renewing their relationship. As Lischer writes:

> That was the beginning of the great thaw between Leonard and me. Our manner of reconciliation reminded me of the way my father and I communicated . . . *through* something else: throwing a ball, catching a fish, planting a tree, but never direct from one heart to another.
>
> We achieved approximations of feeling for one another, with the tacit understanding that the truth between people is cumulative. Everything will be sorted out at some mythical end point. Until then, extended conversation is premature at best.

Had Lischer sought to bring about reconciliation by directly confronting the brokenness, he might have exacerbated the conflict. After all, even in cases where all sides are of good will, there is enormous potential for misunderstanding, distorted communication and intrusive bitterness. Then there are the lurking dangers of power dynamics, the desire to avoid being humiliated and the difficulty of externalizing one's internal pain.

I assigned *Open Secrets* to my class of first-year theological students and looked forward to lecturing on the significance of Christian ministry and, in particular, to emphasizing the significance of the smaller moves and gestures that may open up opportunities to move toward reconciliation.

My preparation for the lecture coincided with the beginning of the U.S. bombings of Afghanistan. Might there be a connection, I wondered, between the national response and how we respond to personal conflicts, division, betrayal? Lischer was writing about an estrangement between friends in an interpersonal setting and about his sense of the cumulative development of truth. The struggles against Osama bin Laden are about a political, international conflict between strangers, indeed enemies—but also about the cumulative development of ideological hatred.

John Paul Lederach is a mediator with 20 years' experience of trying "to effect nonviolent change around the globe where cycles of deep violence seem hell-bent on perpetuating themselves." He says:

> We should be careful to pursue one and only one thing as the strategic guidepost of our response: avoid doing what they expect. What they expect from us is the lashing out of the giant against the weak, the many against the few. This will reinforce their capacity to perpetrate the myth they carefully seek to sustain: that they are under threat, fighting an irrational and mad system that has never taken them seriously and wishes to destroy them and their people. What we need to destroy is their myth, not their people.

This does not mean that we are wrong to offer a forceful response to the terror we endured. But it does suggest that we too quickly respond in kind. Many people's rhetoric of "bombing Afghanistan back to the stone age" reflects the tit-for-tat mentality that fuels cycles of violence and brokenness. Might there be a way of opening a door to reconciliation by indirection, by doing the unexpected? Might this be what Jesus had in mind when he called on disciples to "love your enemies, and pray for those who persecute you"?

To be sure, neither in Lischer's case with Leonard nor in the conflict between the U.S. and terrorist networks can one assume that reconciliation will happen quickly. Lischer describes the shared gesture in ministry as "the beginning of the great thaw." Any thaw that might occur between the U.S. and the people sympathetic to bin Laden will take years, perhaps generations, to develop.

But my lecture that day did focus on the importance of the unexpected small gestures that have the capacity to transform. What might they look like? An invitation to share in a ministry need with a neighbor; Anwar Sadat entering the Knesset; a mother offering an estranged child an unexpected gift; Nelson Mandela opening a horizon for transformed relations by refusing vengeance; a kiss of peace in a setting of worship; Jesus washing his disciples' feet.

Lederach calls people to give birth to the unexpected by responding through indirection. By shifting the dynamics of the situation, relationship or system, we open possibilities for transforming our imaginative landscapes. It requires creativity, subtlety and a capacity to imagine relations that look very different from the ones we are currently experiencing. It also requires an ability to believe in miracles that begin with a small step in a different direction.

November 21–28, 2001

Reflection / Discussion Questions

1. Can you think of an example in your own experience where two people have reconciled a difference because one person thawed the freeze with an unexpected act of kindness, a refusal to perpetuate the hostility? Share your thoughts on this example.
2. Is there a balance to be struck between grace-full responses and responses that seem to accept or even encourage hostile behavior? How would you describe such a balance?
3. Many years after Jacob's trickery against Esau, Jacob returned again to meet his brother and was understandably nervous about the reunion. Read about their encounter in Genesis 32:1–33:11 and compare Esau's reaction to his previous feelings in Genesis 27:41.
4. Are there rifts in your relationships or among members of your congregation? What kinds of grace-full gestures might enable reconciliation to occur?

8

VOCATION

DURING MY FIRST year of teaching, I learned the hazards of asking college seniors their postgraduation plans. I had mistakenly thought that a good way of getting to know the senior students in my spring seminar would be to ask them about their future. Instead of hearing about plans, I received anxious and concerned looks combined with tentatively spoken hopes and uncertainties. Only a couple of the students were clear about what they would be doing.

As I witness more and more high school, college and seminary graduation exercises, I find that the theme of jobs and vocation keeps recurring. Many students are still uncertain about their vocations. While this is understandably true of high school graduates, it is also true of many college graduates and even of some graduating from professional school. The clearest exceptions are those "second-career" students who have returned to school in order to pursue another vocation.

Is the uncertainty a sign of our changing economic culture? Does it reflect the opening of more opportunities to groups of people who had previously been denied access? Does it indicate a breakdown of communities that provided a clearer "calling" to people? Or some combination of these factors?

Regardless of the causes, many people are searching for guidance in discerning what they ought to do with their lives. In part, the question of vocation has to do with a job. But it also raises important and related issues about marriage and parenting, about the communities and traditions to which we feel accountable in some measure, and about the ways we seek to understand the contingent events of our lives, events that often transform—if not transmute—our plans and our understanding.

How do I discern my vocation over time? We find some guidance from a character in Gail Godwin's *Evensong* who, in affirming the vocation of a woman Episcopal priest, tells her: "Something's your vocation if it keeps making more of you." Part of what distinguishes vocation from simply tasks or work that needs to be done is the conviction that the activity is an ingredient in a faithful, flourishing life. We aim for commitments that generate and discipline our passion and thereby continually make more of us than if we failed to participate in that way of life.

Conversely, we ought to avoid those vocations that are likely to make "less" of us, especially if in them we are likely to be shriveled by one or another form of sin. We can be made "less" by our own temptations, by a particular mismatch between what we are doing and the gifts we have been given by God, by contingent events that overwhelm the possibilities of continuing a specific vocation, or by the corrupting practices or institutions that currently shape our vocation.

Godwin's phrase helps orient us toward vocations that encourage a flourishing life. But that phrase "more of you" can be co-opted by a seductive culture of self-fulfillment. To avoid that, we need the specificity of Christian communities to guide us in discerning how our vocation is consistent with Christian discipleship. In this sense, Godwin's phrase needs to be placed next to Dietrich Bonhoeffer's claim in *The Cost of Discipleship* that "when Christ calls [someone], He bids him come and die."

After all, even as we recognize the potential for fulfillment and abundant living, Christians recognize that the God whom we worship tells us that only those who lose their life will find it. Further, Christ died on a cross, and Christians have long recognized martyrdom as a sign of faithfulness and sanctity. Littleton's teenager Cassie Bernall discovered a vocation that "made more" of her precisely through death, as did Bonhoeffer a half-century earlier.

Christians ought to be wary of a life in which one finds opportunities or external rewards continually expanding without entailing any personal sacrifice—especially when those rewards come at the expense of others.

Hence, we need to help one another discover vocations in which more will be made of us, enabling us to find fulfillment, even as we also recognize the significant sacrifice involved in faithful Christian discipleship. In this way, we seek to discern and live out vocations that enable people to match their gifts and talents with fidelity to the God of Jesus Christ and particular communities of people.

But how do we engage in such ongoing discernment? How do we live with the tensions of our own faithful and sinful desires, the constraints and opportunities we discover in specific communities and institutions, the twists and turns of our own lives as well as the lives of those we love? We need some clarity of direction as well as an awareness that God often leads us to places we did not plan to go. A familiar joke puts it: "Want to make God laugh? Tell God your plans."

Can we sustain ourselves with a sense of direction oriented by God's inbreaking reign and providential care, enabling us to move forward in our vocational journey with a sense of direction but without a set of predetermined plans? In her wonderful new memoir, *Dance Lessons,* Catherine Wallace insightfully and humorously recalls her discovery of an expansive vocation in relation to God only through the frustrations of unjust academic institutions and the complexities of family life.

Such lessons are more easily narrated retrospectively than they are communicated to graduates and others who are seeking assurance that they are making wise vocational choices. Yet we, their friends, families and Christian communities, are called to help provide them with perspective—with direction shaped by our commitment to God, and with an ironic sense of humor as we discover the surprises that God has in store for us all.

July 14–21, 1999

Reflection / Discussion Questions

1. The English word *vocation* comes from the Latin word for "call." What do you think is your vocation, or calling, in life? How would you describe it to others?

2. God uses people in many capacities to preserve and promote the institutions of God's earthly creation. The children of Adam and Eve have been entrusted with the stewardship of God's creation. How does it affect the way that you do your daily work in the world to think of yourself as being in God's service?

3. In 1 Corinthians 12:4-11, Paul describes some different spiritual gifts by means of which God seeks to build up the Christian community. Each manifestation of the Spirit is given for the common good, and no one is more valuable than another. What gifts do you have that can be used in service of the common good? What can your congregation do to foster an environment wherein each member is encouraged to participate more fully in the common life and work of the church?

9

GOING AND STAYING

ABRAHAM haunts me. The Letter of James calls him a "friend of God"; Paul claims we are Abraham's descendants, heirs according to the promise given to him; Abraham and Sarah are our forebears in the faith. I like being included in such company—yet Abraham haunts me.

I just do not understand the decisiveness with which Abraham responded to the call of God. Nine words near the beginning of chapter 12 in Genesis are stark: "So Abram went, as the Lord had told him. . . ." God offered wonderful promises, but the truth is they were pretty vague. Abraham could not be sure where he was headed; he was told only that it was a land the Lord would show him. He was assured that his name would be a blessing, that the Lord would make of him a great nation.

Given how we see Abraham acting in other contexts, we would expect him to ask: What do you mean by blessing? What kind of nation are we talking about? Just how are you going to make this happen? Could you show me a map of this land? Who is going to pack up the tents?

Abraham does not ask any questions. He goes, trusting in God for the future.

This same pattern characterizes the calling of disciples at the beginning of Mark's Gospel. Jesus calls them while they are fishing, and immediately they leave their nets and follow him. No questions asked, no hesitations offered. One can only imagine what must have been going through their father Zebedee's mind as he watched his sons abandon not only their fishing but also him.

I am haunted by Abraham's and the disciples' decisiveness. They are called, they respond. Their response even seems right. Their decisiveness displays a spontaneity and a willingness to trust God that challenges those of us more inclined to sit, watch and wait for a careful long-range planning projection. I look for ways to make the stories more complex. Surely these people must have asked more questions, expressed greater hesitation. But I know such strategies are a part of my attempt to avoid a lurking, discomforting sense that I ought to be more faithful in responding than I am.

Abraham has haunted me recently because I have had to respond and move. Our family moved this past summer, and it took us forever. My wife and I are both United Methodist ministers, so one would think we would be used to moving by now. But it never gets any easier. In part, this is because we have so much stuff to be packed every time we move.

That stuff burdens us and makes us less mobile. I have new appreciation for the rich young ruler, who becomes very sad when Jesus tells him to sell his possessions and give them to the poor, and then to come and follow him. I understand the rich young ruler's predicament. I do not think Jesus was against possessions; they can be instruments of faithfulness. However, Jesus knew also that possessions can become idols and thus undermine discipleship. That is the rich young ruler's problem.

I like to think that I need all this stuff in order to be of service, to be faithful in my vocation. Surely my books, for example, are a means by which my desire to know and love God and to serve God's people is nurtured and deepened. But I am given pause for reflection when I have to pack and unpack those books, and I discover in very specific terms just how much my family's possessions weigh. Yet why have I found it so difficult to give away books, or to part with other possessions, in the process of moving? Do I have a sinful attachment to things? In the future will my ability, or even my willingness, to discern God's call be inhibited by my desire not to have to move again?

I think that God's call can require an appropriate fidelity to a sense of place. After all, Abraham was not told to move simply because moving is better than staying where you are; he moved in order to provide a people with a place, a land, they could call home. For people who have had to live as nomads, who have always been on the move because of some "other" determining where they can be, that land—that sense of home—is enormously significant. It is part of what makes the contemporary plight of Palestinians in relation to that "land" of Abraham so painful and urgent.

Yet those of us who have found a home in secure national borders, whose sense of place is all too carefully delimited and marked by spaces designed to exclude others, need to be reminded of the significance and power of moving to other lands. For in those other lands we are rendered vulnerable. We can learn there to accept the hospitality of strangers and to discover that there are other ways of doing things than those to which we have become accustomed. To be ready for such a move, we cannot be tied to possessions.

So I remain haunted by Abraham, reminded both of a decisive willingness to go where God calls and of the powerful significance of a specific land that offers us a sense of place. During the move, my possessions were more important than ever to me. I suspect this was because, in the absence of a settled house or community, they substituted for a sense of place. But maybe that is just another way for me to explain my peculiar attachment to loving things more than God rather than using things only insofar as they are conducive to loving God. Perhaps Abraham haunts me because I hear, all too clearly, a call to repentance.

September 10–17, 1997

Reflection / Discussion Questions

1. When was the last time you moved from one home to another? Did you feel unsettled or out of place? How was the move related to your sense of vocation?
2. Do you think that your possessions foster a love of *things* or are they conducive to loving *God*? Explain. Should you buy fewer things than you do? Will you?
3. A walk through any shopping mall or a critical observation of most advertisements will quickly reveal our society's patterns of excessive personal consumption. How can you and your congregation act as Christian agents of change in our possession-driven culture?
4. Read Genesis 12:1-4 and Mark 5:1-20. God called Abraham to leave everything familiar and to go to a new place. When Jesus healed the Gerasene demoniac in Mark 5, he ordered him to go back home to tell his family and friends about the Lord's mercy. God's call for each of our lives comes with different details, but God is always seeking our allegiance and obedience. Is God calling you to move in any new directions; and if so, in what ways? What obstacles are in your way?

10

MATURING DOWNWARD

W HAT ARE your ambitions?" an administrative colleague asked me recently. I am not often speechless, but this time I didn't know what to say. I briefly considered explaining my understanding of vocation, especially in relation to my primary identity as an ordained minister of the gospel. That would make clear why I have presumed that the church has a legitimate claim on my life. It might also explain why I think less in terms of ambition for a career than faithfulness to a vocation.

I doubted that he wanted that kind of answer. So I responded that I assumed I would return to teaching fulltime. I could tell that he was looking for something more. My friend looked puzzled and was surprised that I hadn't thought more clearly about my ambitions.

I wondered why I had been startled by a straightforward question. Unexpected clarity about my discomfort came later that day. A student who has become a friend had written a reflection on the death of a mutual friend, a faithful and impressive Christian. Here's what he wrote: "He had rocketed upward from a prestigious Oxford scholarship to a spectacular academic career to a prominent national platform. But as John began to internalize weakness, and then grace, he gradually matured downward. As far as success is defined, John had chosen to make himself irrelevant."

He gradually matured downward. . . . Those words seem

odd in a culture defined by upward mobility, career ladders and unbridled ambition. Yet they are peculiarly appropriate to following One who came to serve rather than be served, who said we would have to lose our lives in order to find them.

Yet as beautiful and truthful as John's life was, I found the clarity fading and my puzzlement returning. I realized that I was uncomfortable with the assumptions of downward mobility. Are all of us called to maturing downward? Is there any place for the appropriate use of power, of office?

Surely in the diversity of gifts given by God, not all are called to the faithful, simple yet difficult life of cultural or ecclesiastical "irrelevance." But neither are we called to define ourselves by cultural assumptions about success and upward mobility. If ambition denotes and inspires a striving for excellence, then should we not be hoping for people who are ambitious for the gospel?

Interestingly, in both James and Philippians we are enjoined against pursuing "selfish ambition." This would seem to suggest that there is a selfless ambition—or, perhaps more accurately, an ambition that strives to resist selfishness in the hope of learning to become selfless.

This is difficult psychological, moral and theological territory. There is enormous potential for self-deception, and there are deeply troubling consequences of people who trample others in the pursuit of self-aggrandizing power clothed in false humility. This is particularly galling—and dangerous—when done in the name of Christ.

In the Letter of James, selfish ambition is linked to envy, and both produce "disorder and wickedness of every kind." They are part of a false wisdom "from below." By contrast, "the wisdom from above is first pure, then peaceable, gentle, willing to yield, full of mercy and good fruits, without a trace of partiality or hypocrisy" (3:16-17).

James recognizes the dangers of self-deception. He suggests that we cannot seek both selfish ambition and the wisdom from above; we cannot be simultaneously a friend of the world and a friend of God. Rather, by focusing our lives and our ambition on serving God faithfully, we equip ourselves to serve in the world with integrity.

Similarly, Philippians calls followers of Christ to reject selfish ambition. Here Paul is clearly concerned about selfishness, but also about shaping a common life marked by Christ. He writes, "Be of the same mind, having the same love, being in full accord and of one mind. Do nothing from selfish ambition or conceit, but in humility regard others as better than yourselves. Let each of you look not to your own interests, but to the interests of others. Let the same mind be in you that was in Christ Jesus . . ." (2:2b-5). The paradigm, Paul suggests, is following Christ, whose life is marked by self-emptying, by humility, by obedience.

Can ambition coexist with self-emptying, humility, obedience? If we try to moderate our ambition with altruism, ambition will win and self-deception will intensify.

Rather, we need a transformation of what we desire, what we aspire to and count as important. Our lives are to be focused on Christ and appropriate, faithful service to Christ. In order to unlearn sin—including bitter envy and selfish ambition—and learn the ways of holy living, we need to cultivate a common life with others in Christian community. Our brothers and sisters in Christ become resources for us, offering both support and challenge in discerning how to serve Christ most faithfully. And we become resources for them. The task is to cultivate the same mind that was in Christ Jesus, maintaining a consistent vigilance against bitter envy and selfish ambition—and against the ennui that can set in if and when others seem more successful by the standards of the world.

For some people, like my friend John, cultivating the mind of Christ in community involves gradually maturing downward. For others, it may mean a willingness to serve in positions the world counts as successful. But in either case, the call is to measure ourselves not by worldly stature or success, but by our fidelity to Christ. Easier said than done.

August 29–September 5, 2001

Reflection / Discussion Questions

1. Many of us measure our success in dollars and cents. Others measure it by professional title, academic degree, or public approval. How do you measure success?
2. When James and John asked Jesus to sit at his right and left hand in glory, Jesus responded with an illustration about positions of honor (Mark 10:35-45). The Gentile rulers "lord it over" one another, Jesus says; but his prescription for the Christian community is abruptly simple: "Not so among you." The temptation to seek positions of honor and authority for their own sake, or to clutch onto power, is insidious. What can we Christians do to establish other priorities for ourselves?
3. God has continued since biblical times to call and use people in positions of power, wealth, and influence. If you find yourself serving God from a position that the world counts as successful, what can you do to prioritize faithfulness to vocation over career ambition?

PART 2

FRIENDS
AND MENTORS

11

SHAPING CHARACTER

A SEMINARY STUDENT and I were walking around the lake on a beautiful evening. We had begun the walk in part for exercise, and in part because he wanted to talk about his vocation. He had begun to think seriously about his ministerial identity, his spiritual formation, and the oscillating sense of excitement and apprehension he felt about how others would perceive him as "the minister."

We had a stimulating and wide-ranging conversation about the church, seminary life and the challenges seminaries face with issues of formation, education and malformation. We discussed the importance of spiritual discipline and the ways in which the student would need to develop practices and habits of prayer in order to sustain his strong commitment to a ministry of social justice.

Toward the end of the conversation, he shifted the topic to an issue specific to his formation: marriage. How do you know, he wondered aloud, when you have discovered the best person to marry? I quickly responded that you never really know for sure—marriage is a commitment you make in faith and hope and love. He said he understood all that; he didn't mean "know" in the sense of certainty. I realized that he was asking how, amid the many uncertainties of life, you discover that a particular person is the one with whom you will make a lifelong commitment.

The student followed his initial question with one that got

specific and personal: how had I concluded that my wife was the person I wanted to marry? I somewhat nervously offered a series of quips designed to deflect the question. But I also realized that I owed him a response equal to the thoughtfulness and seriousness of his concern.

I began with the obvious. You need to be sure that you are attracted to the person and that you enjoy spending time with that person. There should be a basic compatibility. However, a good marriage needs to go much deeper than that.

I paused. How does one describe depth? I recalled the dynamics of my own marriage, and the ways in which that commitment had enabled me to change and grow over the 16 years since I was in the student's situation. In that light, I suggested that in marriage, you are making a determination about the kind of person who will significantly shape your character amid the vicissitudes of life.

Alas, the student wanted me to say more. And I felt the burden of saying something thoughtful, something more than a banal truism about the risks of making any commitment. I thought about character and about why I am so sure now that marrying my wife was critical to my own Christian formation.

Finally, I said: You should want to marry someone who will challenge the vices you have come to love and affirm the gifts you are afraid to claim. We both sensed that I had stumbled onto a formulation that was worth further reflection, but we decided to pursue it on another occasion.

What was I trying to say in that formulation? Perhaps that it seems obvious that we would be drawn to people who reflect and reinforce our vices as well as our virtues. They provide us with a strong comfort zone. Further, it seems clear that insofar as we want to be challenged and encouraged, we typically want to be challenged to give up those vices we already hate and be encouraged to enhance those gifts we already exemplify.

It seems less obvious that we would want to live with someone who would challenge us to give up the vices we love and to affirm the gifts we are afraid to claim. But this is where our real growth in character will occur. This kind of challenge is also crucial to nourishing a healthy marriage.

To be sure, such growth involves commitment, takes time and requires trust. It involves a commitment that we will give of our own lives sufficiently to allow that relationship to shape our character. It takes time for us to believe that another person understands us well enough to know where our real vices and gifts are to be found. It also requires trust that the other person genuinely wants us to grow, that the challenge and affirmation the other offers are not primarily self-interested or a reflection of competitive power dynamics.

This trust can be cultivated only if the challenge is also balanced by the affirmation. We know of relationships where people consistently challenge only our vices (both those we hate and those we love), and we avoid them because they are excessively critical. We also need affirmation of who we are and who we might become if we claimed the gifts that others discern in us.

No one can predict the joys and griefs, the hopes and fears, the expected and unexpected circumstances that undoubtedly affect the dynamics of a particular marriage. Amid those uncertainties, however, we can seek to discern those qualities in another person that will help guide us through life. Of course, this is not unique to marriage. We hope that close friends will also challenge our vices and affirm our gifts. Even more, we long to discover committed Christian communities that offer such support and challenge.

I realized that the two primary analogies I was thinking about were my own marriage and the patterns of Wesleyan class meetings. In both settings, challenge and support offer a paradigm for growth in Christian life.

It is never easy to expose ourselves to being challenged to give up our vices and to claim our gifts. Yet we are invited to do so in and through commitment to such relationships as marriage, friendship and Christian community. Such relationships are a school where we learn what it means to love God as God has first loved us. Our commitment shapes our character, even as our character shapes our commitment. That may not make the risk of commitment easier, but it provides a context for helping us discover its life-giving potential.

December 23–30, 1998

Reflection / Discussion Questions

1. What emotions are evoked for you by the word *challenge*? Does it make you nervous or energize you or both? How do you feel about the word *support*?
2. King David and the prophet Nathan had a relationship of trust. Read 2 Samuel 7 to see the *support* that Nathan offers David and the trust that David exhibits when Nathan reports a different word from the Lord—that the Lord does not want David to build the Temple. Read also 2 Samuel 12, where Nathan has to *challenge* David about his sins against Bathsheba and Uriah. How do you think these two incidents are related? What do they tell you about the relationship between support and challenge?
3. "You should want to marry someone who will challenge the vices you have come to love and affirm the gifts you are afraid to claim." How do you respond to people who challenge your vices? Does it depend on exactly what they are challenging? Does it depend on your relationship with that person? Does it depend on how you perceive

that person's motives? How does your reaction depend on all these things?

4. Are you able to offer both challenge and support to other people? Reflecting on your own reactions to words of challenge and support, what can you learn about offering such words to others?

12

APPRENTICESHIP

A̶T AGE 51, Noah Adams abruptly decided he had to have a piano. He didn't know how to play, but he thought that buying one would compel him to learn. He didn't just buy an old clunker, or even an inexpensive new one. He invested in a new Steinway upright—a financial commitment that provided extra incentive to practice.

Why does someone decide, as a mature adult, to take up a new activity that involves a steep learning curve? Adams, a host on National Public Radio, gives his account in *Piano Lessons,* a delightful memoir of his first year of learning to play. He had long been intrigued with music's evocative power, and he had become particularly enchanted by watching and interviewing piano players of diverse styles. He loved the beauty of their music, the power of their hands and arms gliding across the keys, the gift they offer to their audiences.

Yet learning to play was a daunting task, particularly given his already demanding schedule. Not surprisingly, Adams found it difficult and frustrating; he couldn't simply sit down and make the beautiful music he wanted. There were scales to learn, and basic rhythms to be mastered. Initially, he decided against going to a teacher, trying such shortcuts as a "Miracle Piano Teaching System" on the computer. A friend's warning proved to be prophetic: "You might be learning music with that computer, but you're not learning how to play."

Eventually, Adams signed up for an intensive ten-day music camp. He discovered that there is no substitute for regular, disciplined practice and the tutelage of teachers. By the end of the first year, his frustrations began to recede. He actually desired time for practice. He had become initiated into the art of piano playing. He also learned to appreciate the craft of making and caring for pianos, as well as the importance of the history of pianos and great pianists—classical, jazz, blues, even rock-and-roll.

Just as Adams decided to take up the piano as an adult, so many adults these days are deciding to seek out the church. Some have had childhood lessons in being a Christian, but left the church for many years. Many people who are taking up the church have had little if any exposure to the Christian faith. They are searching, sometimes unaware of what exactly they are hoping to find. How can they learn to practice Christianity?

One temptation is to look for shortcuts, a "Miracle Christian Teaching System." To be sure, new technologies and insights can offer important ways to attract people to the faith. But shortcuts are not likely to teach us the truth about God and ourselves. There is no substitute for the slow, sometimes painful growth that comes through disciplined habits of practice shaped by the grace of the crucified and risen Christ. One does not become an excellent piano player, painter or a soccer star overnight; neither does one learn to become a Christian overnight. One needs teachers and mentors.

In the early church, catechetical practices shaped the initiation of adults into Christian faith and life. Reflection on these practices stirred the imagination of Dietrich Bonhoeffer, who in the face of an acculturated and coopted Christianity sought to reclaim spiritual disciplines, the insights of "the discipline of the secret." They also provide the backdrop for the Roman Catholic Church's Rite for the

Christian Initiation of Adults. Some of these practices—learning the Lord's Prayer and the Apostles' Creed, renouncing evil and resisting injustice, singing praise to God, participating in the Lord's Supper—might seem alien and frustrating at first, similar to what Adams experienced in starting with the piano. Yet, guided by teachers and mentors, such practices foster life-giving and renewing habits that change people's lives.

Those already on the path of Christian discipleship often discover that teaching others helps to renew their own learning. On one level, this is true of teaching anything. As a woman commented to Adams, "Music is such a living thing. I think you learn so much about yourself sitting at the keyboard, and I'm constantly learning just by teaching."

St. Augustine described teaching and learning in similar terms. "So great is the power of sympathy, that when people are affected by us as we speak and we by them as they learn, we dwell in the other and thus both they, as it were, speak in us what they hear, while we, in some way, learn in them what we teach." We do this particularly because, as Augustine elsewhere notes, Christ is the true Teacher from whom all of us—teachers, mentors, students, apprentices—continue to learn by God's grace. Christian formation is a lifelong task for all of us.

Even so, might not the catechumenate seem too "heavy," too "disciplined," for contemporary seekers? To be sure, even in the early church it was only over time that people became comfortable with particular practices of Christian life. We can learn from the example of Adams's piano lessons. He began by simply trying to learn the basics so he could eventually play one piece of music as a gift to his wife. This did not dramatically change his schedule, much less his life. But he gradually began to discover that he wanted to play whenever he could, and these desires began to transform his priorities and his life.

In the Christian life, too, we do not need to try to do

everything all at once. We can take one step at a time, through the guidance of others in the church who help nurture us and educate our desires. As we apprentice ourselves to others, and learn also to offer apprenticeship to others, we can discover (again?) the excitement and the passion for faithful living before God.

July 16–23, 1997

Reflection / Discussion Questions

1. Have you ever developed a skill like piano playing or distance running that takes long-term, disciplined effort to master? Provide some details about this process. Compare the satisfaction of such an accomplishment with something that you acquired more easily.
2. The apostle Paul had several missionary partners on his journeys, and the young Timothy was one of them. First Timothy 4 contains Paul's advice to Timothy while Timothy was a teacher and a pastor to the Christians at Ephesus. Read 1 Timothy 4 and describe the characteristics that Paul admonishes Timothy to develop.
3. Some Christians form intentional friendships both with people who can mentor them in the faith and with newer Christians or unbelievers whom they themselves can help to grow. Do you have any relationships like this? If so, briefly describe one or more of them. What new friendships can you make that will help you and others to grow in discipleship to Jesus Christ?
4. What steps can your congregation take to become a place that not only welcomes newcomers but also intentionally helps them to grow in faith, understanding, and love?

13

TAKING THE LONG VIEW

How DO YOU LEARN to think about the long-range implications of issues in a culture that is fixated on the short term? This question kept recurring to me in the midst of very different conversations recently.

The first conversation was about parenting and the character formation of children and youth. The good news, one person reported, is that a recent survey indicated that the vast majority of children interviewed identify one or both of their parents as their primary hero and role model in life.

But, another responded, "Is that really good news? Too many parents have lost sight of what it means to form children's character. These days, parents are so busy with their own lives that they look for short-term fixes without regard for the good habits that children need for shaping good character. And then they justify their cop-out by distinguishing their relationship as 'quality rather than quantity' time. Give me a break."

There is no substitute for the quantity of time we spend with our children. We ought to hope that it is also quality time, but we cannot afford to contrast one with the other. In a world where we put instant coffee into microwave ovens and are impatient at how long it takes to warm up, is it any wonder that we have commodified time and become preoccupied with "quality" at the expense of "quantity" time with our children?

When I recently asked my kids what they would most like for me to change in our relationship, each one independently asked for more time together. I do a reasonably good job of maintaining a day-to-day relationship with them, yet I am also acutely aware of my own temptation to do whatever I can to make life easier—on them and on me—rather than to focus on what is needed for the cultivation of character over the long term.

After all, character can be formed only over time. Character identifies that which we most value in life, and it reflects the long-term formation of our emotional, moral and intellectual lives. As Aristotle rightly insisted, character is formed through shaping habits of life through disciplined practice and the cultivation of morally significant friendships. And, particularly with children, there is no substitute for sustained presence over time.

A few days after this conversation about parenting, my wife and I were at dinner with a quite different group of people. Here the conversation focused on the prospect of North Carolina's approving a lottery as a way to deal with looming budget deficits. Most of those gathered were opposed to the lottery, and we rehearsed many of the familiar reasons for concern: its impact on the poor, the possible involvement of organized crime, and our inability to make the hard political decisions about the common good without the "easy money" that a lottery provides.

Yet, recalling my earlier conversation about the "quick-fix," short-term approach to parenting, I wondered whether the deeper problem with the lottery is that it encourages illusions of a personal quick fix to long-term economic issues. It is a commonplace that politics is inevitably preoccupied with the short term, but I wondered whether the lottery didn't corrode the long-term issues of forming worthy character. How do we begin to shape such virtues as prudence, honesty, courage and patience if we create illusions that anyone can—and perhaps will—win the lottery?

Is this perhaps the logical extension of a dominant, amoral approach to economic and political life? Richard Sennett thinks so, and has written a polemical critique of "the new, flexible capitalism" and its impact on character. At the beginning of *The Corrosion of Character*, Sennett poses some powerful questions: "How do we decide what is of lasting value in ourselves in a society which is impatient, which focuses on the immediate moment? How can long-term goals be pursued in an economy devoted to the short term? How can mutual loyalties and commitments be sustained in institutions which are constantly breaking apart or continually being redesigned?"

Sennett's questions seem particularly poignant in light of my conversations about parenting and the lottery. They also point to the urgent need for the church to reclaim more focused attention on the long-term challenges of shaping character. If we want to bear witness to the gospel of forgiveness that offers new life, we must become skilled at cultivating patience, especially in a world that tries to make us ever more impatient.

But are we ready to take the long view? Can we really come to terms with a God who is patient, slow to anger, abounding in mercy and steadfast love? Are we willing to acknowledge that the making of disciples takes time? That perhaps one of the central reasons for the Bible's preoccupation with such issues as idolatry and greed has to do with the ways in which we search for fantasies to avoid the hard work of patiently shaping a holy character over time?

Even more, are we in the church willing to acknowledge that we need to be more attentive, and involved, in the parenting of children—in churches, in schools, in activities? Why is it that the same parents who are so willing to spend hour upon hour going to soccer practices are so resistant to expectations for a serious confirmation process?

Are we in the church willing to confront the illusions of lotteries, and to challenge the presumptions of short-term economic thinking? Are we willing to tackle the hard questions of what we ought to expect financially from one another in order to cultivate a genuinely common good over the long-term? Or is the quick fix still in?

April 11, 2001

Reflection / Discussion Questions

1. What priorities do you have for your life for the next five, ten, twenty, or fifty years? How are you making decisions now that will affect such a long-term future? Are there short-term costs associated with your long-term goals? Explain.
2. What similar priorities can you identify for your congregation or for other communities in which you are involved?
3. Read Matthew 6:19-21 and identify the things in your life that might be "treasures on earth" and "treasures in heaven." What will last and what will pass away? As you think about this, consider the words of the twentieth-century missionary and martyr Jim Elliott, who paraphrased these verses from Matthew 6: "He is no fool who gives what he cannot keep, to gain what he cannot lose."
4. Think, pray, and talk about discerning God's long-term priorities for you and your community. How can you and your community live more consistently with those priorities?

14

STORIES OF OUR LIVES

I HAVE OFTEN been compared to my father. Though I neither look nor sound like him, I seem to have his temperament, some of his intellectual gifts and some of his vices. We have also followed a similar trajectory in our vocations.

These comparisons and references have increased over the past year, since he is one of my predecessors as dean of Duke Divinity School. He had served as dean for only 18 months when, in July 1982, he died suddenly of a heart attack.

I have often reflected on the unexpected ways in which our lives have continued to intersect even after his death. In my current position, I frequently encounter friends, colleagues and acquaintances of my father. They tell me stories about participating with him in the Methodist Student Movement or sharing caravan trips of young adults. Some speak appreciatively of his years as editor of *motive* magazine, while others recall him as a preacher and teacher. Through their stories, I have learned a lot about my father's life as a youth and young adult—stories I had hoped I would one day hear him tell.

Just last month I encountered a story written by my father that I did not know existed. It was given to me by my wife's brother. He never met my father, but he found in a used bookstore a collection of essays titled *Highways to Faith: Autobiographies of Protestant Christians* (1954) that includes an essay "Doing Changes Living," by Jameson Jones.

I was surprised to discover this story, not least because my father was always reticent about himself and his faith. I have always regretted not having the opportunity to sit down with him for a long talk about his growing-up years, the kind of conversation I was privileged to have with each of my grandfathers. But I also knew that my father would likely have deflected any such conversation, indicating that others' lives were more worthy of reflection than his own.

I have come to share that emphasis on telling the lives of saintly others. In this era of television talk shows and countless "as told to" autobiographies, we are afflicted by too many people who think their lives are infinitely more interesting than they are. This is a problem that also tempts preachers. Too many sermons seem designed to glorify the preacher's life rather than God. I want to hear less about the preacher and more about God and the transformative power of the gospel.

Even so, there are people whose life stories are interesting and compelling. Their autobiographies offer us significant resources for loving and knowing God more faithfully and truthfully. But the power of autobiography for such purposes depends significantly on how the story is told. Contrast, for example, the "confessions" written by Augustine with those written by Rousseau: Augustine gives an account of his life by drawing attention to God, whereas Rousseau draws attention to himself. Indeed, Rousseau deliberately crafts a counternarrative to Augustine's, shifting the focus of the story from God to the self. Rousseau is the patron saint of modern autobiography.

I am wary of autobiographies precisely because of such self-centeredness. That has been intensified by the ways in which television and pop best sellers have sensationalized and trivialized the difficult task of autobiography. In our time, even those who seek to praise God through the telling of their stories often inadvertently end up giving God second-billing.

Yet there remains something powerful and compelling about hearing people tell the stories of their own lives. I am grateful to have discovered—even 16 years after his death—that my otherwise reticent father had, at least on one occasion, told the story of how God was working in his life.

I recently attended a consultation on "the vocation of theological teachers." As the participants described diverse senses of vocation, and how vocation had shaped their identities as scholars, teachers, parents, pastors and friends, we found ourselves telling stories. Some of the stories were from our own lives, while others were about saintly mentors whose encouragement at pivotal times had enabled us to go on.

During those conversations, several people expressed wariness about becoming self-indulgent in our storytelling—a wariness with which I resonated. At the same time, however, I was convinced it was important to tell our stories in the context of our consultation—to identify how God had been working in our lives to shape our vocations as theological teachers. Such storytelling reveals the interrelated webs that constitute the fabric of our lives and locates us in the larger drama of God's journey with God's people.

I continue to believe that Christians ought to be wary of autobiography, particularly in a culture that gives us ample opportunities for self-indulgence. There is an appropriate—indeed, crucial—sense in which we ought to focus our attention on God and on the role of saintly mentors. We ought to lift up, in our congregations and in our culture, the stories of those who enable us to see God and the transformative power of the gospel more clearly and faithfully.

Even so, we ought not fail to tell the story of our lives to and with one another. As Augustine's *Confessions* so powerfully teaches us, we can reflect on our own lives in ways that reveal the gifts God has given to us, help others understand our vocations, and draw attention to saintly mentors whose lives have made such a crucial difference in our own. The real question is not whether we tell the story of our lives. It is whether we will do so in ways faithful to our vocation to love and know God in all that we are and do.

October 21, 1998

Reflection / Discussion Questions

1. Do you know the stories of your parents' lives? If so, how are you like or unlike them? What have you needed to unlearn in order to be your own person?

2. Can you think of people who tend to live in such a way as to point away from themselves to others and to God? Can you think of people who tend to draw attention instead to themselves? What do you think is the difference? How can you take steps to be more like the former?

3. Read John 3:22-35 and consider how John the Baptist described his own life and purpose in relation to Jesus. Think about how you might tell the story of your own life in a way that does not draw attention to yourself, either by self-aggrandizement or self-deprecation. How can you tell your story so that it is genuinely in the praise of God?

4. Public leaders sometimes talk about "institutional memory," that is, a community's memory of its collective past. What has been the historical character of your congregation? In what specific ways has it borne witness to its God and Savior? How can the recollection and telling of memories shape your congregation's present ministry and its witness?

15

ONE GOOD TEACHER

W̲E BURIED a fine teacher the other day. He was not a scintillating lecturer, nor was he a particularly exciting person. But he was an excellent scholar, and his passion for his subject matter, for the life of the mind and for his students all shone forth brilliantly. As I looked out over the congregation gathered for his memorial service, I saw students who had traveled long distances to remember him, and recalled the difference he had made in many people's lives.

Henry Adams said, "A teacher affects eternity; he can never tell where his influence stops." I read those words in *Tuesdays with Morrie,* Mitch Albom's beautiful tribute to one of his teachers. Twenty years after he had graduated from college, long after he had stopped having any regular contact with Morrie Schwartz, Albom began to visit his beloved old sociology professor. Why? In part because Morrie was dying, but even more because Albom wanted to reconnect with a person who had played a key role in his life.

Morrie was lucky to have one of his students return to reestablish old ties, and to learn about the difference his teaching had made in Albom's life. Too many teachers live only with the unconfirmed hope that their teaching has made a difference. I never took the time to write and thank one of my best and most beloved teachers, a woman who during my high school years sustained hope in my ability and demanded excellence in me. She rekindled my love for learning at a time when it was close to being extinguished. She helped to change my life.

Over a century and a half ago, Ralph Waldo Emerson wrote in his journal: "The whole secret of the teacher's force lies in the conviction that [people] are convertible. And they are. They want awakening." When we encounter teachers who enable that awakening, who challenge our complacency or our smug self-confidence, we may struggle with the changes that occur—but we also are grateful for the growth. In many cases, teachers shape their students' lives with their passion, dedication and excellence.

Over the past few weeks, I have encountered several short essays bearing witness to the importance of teachers. In *Newsweek*, Robert Samuelson pays tribute to a teacher who not only gave good lectures, but also transmitted "life-changing lessons." In the *New York Times Review of Books*, Andrew Delbanco draws on Emerson's thought to insist that English teachers reclaim the vocation of being professors "in the religious sense of that word—ardent, exemplary, even fanatic."

Both essays inspired me to rededicate myself to the holy significance of teaching, and to give thanks for the wonderful teachers whose commitment, witness and teaching had made such a pivotal difference in my life. I also was inspired to get in touch with some of them to express my appreciation.

Yet even as I have been moved by these positive examples, I am also moved by chemist Robert L. Wolke's testimony to the power of bad teaching. In *The Chronicle of Higher Education,* Wolke argues that too often we assume that "bad teaching can have, at worst, a net educational consequence of zero, inasmuch as it fails to produce any positive effects." He contends that there is such a thing as "negative" teaching—that has a lasting adverse impact on students. He draws on his own experience to make his point, recalling a professor who managed to extinguish, at least for a time, Wolke's interest in a subject.

How many times have we not only missed an opportunity to teach others, but actually extinguished the curiosity, the searching spirit, the openness to intellectual conversion in those entrusted to our care? Teachers occupy a special place of privilege and responsibility, whether they are lecturing at a college, leading an honors seminar at a high school, beginning to acquaint children with the joy of learning at an elementary school, or instructing people in faith at a church.

We have paid insufficient attention to the roles that teachers play within the church, for good and for ill. Pastors are called to teach the faith to their congregations, just as laity teach in a variety of settings. I recall particular people in my own journey who have been extremely important in shaping my understanding of Christian faith and life—a Sunday school youth teacher who made us think and challenged us to grow, a pastor whose immersion in scripture made its pages come alive for me, a layperson whose passion for serving the poor awakened a deeper understanding of the scope of our faith and commitment, a faithful Bible study leader who has been teaching every week for over four decades.

Unfortunately, I also have been all too aware of poor teachers of Christian faith who have not only missed an opportunity to make the faith come alive for students, but have actually extinguished a love for God and the church that may have already been kindled. There may be no more important position in the church than to be a Sunday school teacher—and yet we often offer only the most minimal training, typically because we are so desperate to have the classroom staffed that we are afraid to ask our teachers to do more than be there on Sunday morning.

What if we really believed that teaching makes a difference? What if we really believed not that teaching is at worst an activity with a net educational equivalence of zero, but that it's an activity with the potential to feed the spirit? What if we became convinced that one of the reasons we have such difficulty in maintaining a love for the gospel among our young people is that we have invested so little in teaching them, in cultivating that passion and interest in the first place?

November 17–24, 1999

Reflection / Discussion Questions

1. Think of the teachers you have had in Sunday school, elementary school, high school, or college. How are you indebted to them for shaping the person you are now? Is there a particular teacher to whom you might write a letter of thanks even today? How would you express yourself in this letter?

2. James 3:1 warns us explicitly of the great responsibility that comes with teaching, and Jesus describes a similar situation in Mark 9:42. In what ways do you function as a teacher in your life? What examples do you set for your children, grandchildren, friends, or colleagues? Do these passages from Mark and James cause you to think about your role any differently? How so?

3. One of Jesus' roles on earth was that of a teacher, and the Gospel of Matthew emphasizes this especially. Take time to read Matthew. How can and do you learn from Jesus as teacher?

4. What can you do in your community to be more supportive of teachers and the role they play in shaping our children's future?

16

WRITING IN TIME

SEVERAL YEARS AGO Carly Simon recorded a CD titled "Letters Never Sent." The songs reflect a collection of letters she wrote over the years but never sent to the intended recipients. In an interview, Simon said that she keeps a shoebox on a closet shelf to hold these letters. She finds writing them therapeutic, a way to keep frustrations from bottling up inside her. Yet she has also discovered that while these letters are important to write, they are better left unsent.

Even letters sent in the most righteous spirit of indignation can do more harm than good. We know, from our experiences of speaking in anger or frustration, that we sometimes wish we could retract the words as soon as they are out of our mouths. Letters give us an opportunity to cool down and think through what is better left unsaid. Writing a letter without sending it allows us to "say" what we want or need to say and "get it out of our system" without communicating it to the other.

When do you decide not to send a letter? Perhaps in the process of finding an envelope, addressing it and putting a stamp on it. Or perhaps in the time between writing the letter and actually putting it in the mailbox. Perhaps after a good night's sleep. A wise friend once advised me never to send a difficult letter on the same day I write it.

Yet in an age of e-mail, we find it all too easy to send the messages we have written—including those written in a fit of frustration. The reply and send buttons on the computer are all too available. E-mail resembles the volatility of oral communication more than the thoughtful process of letter writing.

Recent studies have suggested that one effect of e-mail correspondence is a coarsening of communication. We tend to respond more quickly, more bluntly and with less concern for the formality and nuance that soften even the most pointed letter. I know of several e-mail messages that would have been better off left in the "never sent" category. Letter writing is more conducive to practicing the virtue of patience.

On the other hand, there are many letters that I have been meaning to send for a long time, but have never found time to write. They are letters of gratitude, of love, of appreciation to people who have touched my life in significant ways. Somehow the writing of these letters is continually deferred by the press of other duties, by the passionate investments in current issues, conflicts and relationships.

I recently received a letter from a reader in response to my "Faith Matters" column about "one good teacher." He wrote to say that a few years earlier, at Thanksgiving, he had written to thank a beloved college professor for her patient insistence that he become a better writer. She sent him back a card thanking him for his thoughtfulness and indicated that it was the first such letter she had received in over 40 years of teaching.

The reader's letter reminded me of how much my father treasured such letters of appreciation. After he died I was given the responsibility of sorting through his papers and files. In a prominent yet private place, I found a file folder marked "Letters for When I Feel Low." Inside the folder was a collection of letters of friendship, gratitude and affection he had received through the years from a variety of people. Some of the letters were handwritten, others typed. Some were relatively short, others were more like essays. Some were from former parishioners and students, others from current colleagues. Some were from people he had known a short time, and others from lifelong friends. What they had in common was that they touched my father, and collectively they provided a reservoir of testimonies to which he turned when he felt discouraged.

We do not need to send only letters of praise and encouragement. Important letters may also involve constructive criticism, or ongoing discernment about difficult decisions that may, at least initially, be difficult to receive. But the act of writing and receiving letters allows us to express our considered judgments and reactions in ways that build community, giving grace to others rather than merely venting frustration or fomenting evil (see Eph. 4:29; James 3). The stakes are high in written correspondence, for letters leave a potentially permanent legacy of expressed judgments, feelings and reactions.

Christians are blessed to have a range of written correspondence to draw from in the New Testament, each letter useful in its own way for building up the body of Christ. I can imagine the church folks in Philippi putting Paul's letter to them in a "letters for when we feel low" file. On the other hand, the letter to the Galatians offers the kind of constructive criticism and discernment that would no doubt have been difficult to receive. And, judging from some of the comments Paul makes in 2 Corinthians 7, there is some correspondence he might have been better off not sending.

I am not suggesting that we return to only writing and receiving letters. I am an advocate of e-mail and other technologically advanced means of communication—they foster more efficient interaction in many circumstances. But I hope never to lose sight of the power of writing thoughtful and discerning letters. I'll write some letters that I won't send, and some that I'll put in the mail today.

May 17, 2000

Reflection / Discussion Questions

1. Have you ever written any letters you haven't sent? Have you sent letters you wish you hadn't? What letters have you received that have caused a strong reaction in you, either positive or negative?

2. Do you have any old friendships or other relationships that could receive new life if you wrote a letter today? Describe them in some fashion, if you are comfortable doing so.

3. Read the first chapters of Paul's letters to the Galatians and to the Philippians. How do the tones of the openings of these letters reveal the state of the relationship between Paul and each community at the time he wrote the letters?

4. The Bible has sometimes been referred to as God's love letter to humanity. Certainly it contains the wonderful news of the story of Jesus Christ and his life, death, and resurrection for our sake. Although the documents in the Bible were originally written to people long ago, how would it change your reading of the Bible to think of it as a letter of loving news also for you?

5. In 2 Corinthians 3:3, Paul tells the Corinthian Christians that they are a letter from Christ, "written not with ink but with the Spirit of the living God." In your role as a letter from Christ, consider and describe what news or what message you are communicating from God to the people in your world.

17

ROSES FOR MY SOUL

It WAS APRIL 1968. Martin Luther King Jr. had just been assassinated. Many Christians were consumed with grief, and many were beginning to feel a sense of despair. Divisions over race, Vietnam and poverty seemed to be intensifying. Prior to his assassination, even King had begun to doubt whether Christians in the U.S. had the will to repent of racist attitudes and actions.

On the campus of Duke University, the mood was similar. Samuel DuBois Cook was at the time an associate professor of political science, the first tenured African-American faculty member at Duke or at any other predominantly white university in the South. He attended King's funeral as an official representative of Duke University.

During those same days, a silent vigil was held in front of Duke Chapel to protest the continuing injustice on campus and in our land. More than a thousand students, faculty, staff and friends of Duke gathered to bear witness to the promise of social justice and equality, the hope for the creation of "the beloved community." Each night they would light candles to signal that the light continued to shine and that the darkness had not overcome it.

When Dr. Cook returned from King's funeral, he addressed the people gathered at the silent vigil:

The only thing I have to say about my experience at Dr.

King's funeral is that your commitment and behavior here made the occasion more bearable, ethically meaningful, and less tragic. As I saw, from afar, the casket containing his lifeless body, I was sustained by the knowledge of a thousand or more bodies, full of life, vision and integrity, here carrying on his legacy in the spirit and in conformity with his ideals and methods. I was uplifted by the fact that you had made his mission your very own. And I am sure that Martin Luther King would be proud of you—mighty proud of you. Your vigil wiped my tears and helped to sustain me. You provided, at a tragic moment, roses for my soul.

It is tempting, then and now, to give in to despair—whether it is in the face of persistent racism and other ethnic divisions, increasing poverty and the maldistribution of resources around the world, or other social problems and vices that continue to diminish and destroy people's lives.

But there are also people in our midst whose faithful lives provide roses for our souls. Their actions and their words may not make it into our newspapers or onto the evening news. They may not develop policies that dramatically change our prospects for lessening the gaps between the rich and the poor, nor even chart a dramatic vision for the politics of a new America. They may simply sustain the hope of one community, or perhaps several overlapping communities, by their steadfast faithfulness. The novelist George Eliot wrote, "That things are not so ill between thee and me, is half-owing to those who lived faithful lives, and rest in unvisited tombs."

Such people provide hope in the midst of despair, and their lives provide testimony to the power of ordinary, faithful witness. As we look back on the days of the civil rights movement in the 1950s and 1960s, we are tempted to see its accomplishments as the result of some inevitable historical forces. Yet, as I read the first two volumes of Taylor Branch's magisterial account of America during the King years, *Parting the Waters* and *Pillar of Fire*, I have been repeatedly struck by the ways in which extraordinary changes emerged from ordinary, vulnerable people's faithfulness. We know the stories of Rosa Parks and Ruby Bridges. But there are countless others who, in subtle ways, helped to shape history by bearing faithful witness in hope for a better future.

We are now approaching the 30th anniversary of King's assassination. Many of the problems against which King struggled continue to haunt us today; many of them seem more entrenched than ever. It would be easy to become cynical and give in to despair. As one student commented to me, "King should have learned that optimism doesn't pan out in the long run."

Maybe not, but hope does. Hope does not rest on an optimistic assessment of either our world or us. Rather, hope rests on trust in the triumph of God's grace, trust that ultimately God's creative and recreative purpose for our world will be brought to fruition. It is that sort of trust that leads people to undertake a children's march in Birmingham, that leads people to hold a silent vigil in the wake of sinful tragedy, that inspires people to continue to provide faithful witness to the hungry and homeless day by day by day.

A few weeks ago, Duke University inaugurated the Samuel DuBois Cook Society in honor of a man whose life has inspired many. The society is designed to recognize, celebrate and affirm the presence of African-American students, faculty and staff at Duke. Among other activities of the society, each member pledges to serve as a mentor to at least one person of African descent.

Such mentoring will not eradicate racism in American society. But it does promise to make a difference for those involved. Who knows: perhaps in the mentoring process itself new friendships will emerge that challenge our temptations to despair. But perhaps the question for us all, in whatever contexts we find ourselves, is this: in what ways are our lives providing roses for somebody's soul?

April 15, 1998

Reflection / Discussion Questions

1. Do you have any heroes? Who are they? Are they famous or little known? Why do you admire them?
2. There are a number of books that tell the stories of historical Christian saints and martyrs. Find such a book in your church library or favorite bookseller. What can we learn from our forebears?
3. What is the difference between optimism and Christian hope? If "optimism doesn't pan out in the end," why can we still claim that our hope abides (1 Corinthians 13:13) and that it will not disappoint (Romans 5:5)?
4. In Philippians 1:3-11, we read Paul's words from prison to his dear friends in Philippi. What is the nature of their relationship to Paul? Why are they such an encouragement to Paul?
5. Who do you know who is living without hope? In what way can your life provide roses for their soul?

18

RACE AND FRIENDSHIP

O UR SKIN COLOR shouldn't matter. Can't we just be friends?" That was the question a student asked in exasperation as he discovered how he and a fellow student differed on issues of race and the American legal system.

The word "just" is key to the student's plaintive question. It reflects the hope that the two people could somehow transcend racial issues through friendship. But no matter how genuine such hope may be, friendship can be a way to ignore or avoid race. Multiracial friendships may serve to break down racial barriers and foster deeper understandings and relationships, but they may also mask deep racial issues. The illusion may be fostered that since in our personal relationships we can get along with others, racism and ethnic conflicts really are not our problem.

Two recent books seem to take directly opposing tacks on these questions. In *The Trouble with Friendship: Why Americans Can't Think Straight About Race,* Benjamin DeMott contends that Americans cover up social, economic and political issues of racism by invoking the orthodoxy of friendship. He points to "buddy" movies like *White Men Can't Jump, 48 Hours* and *Lethal Weapon,* along with television series such as *The Cosby Show,* as examples of attempts to remove difficult questions of race and racism from public discourse. Such popular themes, fused also into political rhetoric by both Presidents [George H.W.] Bush and

Clinton, suggest that we are conquering racism because we are capable of personal friendships that transcend—or at least ignore—race.

Even a quintessentially political display of racism, such as the beating of Rodney King by officers of the Los Angeles Police Department, was transmuted into a question of personal relationships when King asked the nation, "Can't we just get along?" One can empathize with King's plea. Yet such an appeal tempts us to avoid the complex ways racism infects not simply our personal relationships but entrenched economic and social patterns.

Patricia Raybon tells a different story in *My First White Friend: Confessions on Race, Love, and Forgiveness.* Raybon, an African-American, attributes the beginnings of her transformation on racial issues to a very particular friendship. I was moved by her account, but having read DeMott I had to wonder: had I been seduced by the same illusions that Hollywood and Washington have exploited?

But perhaps Raybon is operating with a different conception of friendship, one that helps us confront rather than avoid the racial issues that grip our lives. She begins by describing how knowledge of the history of white oppression had taught her to hate whites. "Hated them because they had lynched and lied and jailed and poisoned and neglected and discarded and excluded and exploited countless cultures and communities with such blatant intent or indifference as to humanly defy belief or understanding." Sharp, painful, necessary and—given the history—truthful words.

Yet Raybon also came to recognize that her hatred, no matter how legitimate and understandable, was also eating away her self-respect and identity. Her hatred blinded her to authentic gestures of friendship offered by white people—specifically, by a particular white girl in her high school who displayed a "rare" and "shining" kindness. She discovered that, rather than only waiting for whites to seek forgiveness for the injustices done by them, she also needed forgiveness for her hatred and for her inability to see white people in their diverse particularities. In the process Raybon discovered the moral and political significance of friendship.

Multiracial friendships no doubt deserve DeMott's critique so long as they remain at the superficial level of "buddy" movies. But Raybon's witness remains crucial to avoid pessimism and cynicism about race. Her story radiates the transformative power of forgiveness and of friendship, its power to redirect passions and intensify awareness of how the evil called racism continues to afflict our lives and our world.

Churches can and must play a key role in helping people discover such friendship. Christians have done better in talking the talk about combating racism than in walking the walk. Only as we learn to walk together as friends will we discover the skills to deal with entrenched systemic issues. Such friendships undoubtedly will be filled with the pain of our histories, and such pain can drive us away from one another. But as Christians we believe that by learning to be forgiven and to forgive in friendship we are helped to confront and live with the suffering and injustice that grip our lives.

Christians cannot rest content with a description of racism as a "social" problem. Racism is sinful. At the same time, the God whom Christians worship, who has befriended all of humanity in Jesus Christ, refuses to allow us to be trapped by destructive cycles of sin. Consequently, we are all called to befriend one another by the power of the Holy Spirit, unlearning the sin that destroys and divides and learning the possibility of a future not defined by the past. It is not insignificant that Raybon begins her acknowledgments with gratitude to God and "the sweet care of the Holy Spirit" for the blessings on her journey.

Skin color should not matter for friends, but morally significant friendships help us discover why we cannot "just" be friends. None of our friendships is free of larger questions of race, of class, of gender, of sin—at least on this side of the fullness of God's kingdom. Yet because God has befriended us as sinners, Christians have been given the means through friendship to be faithful witnesses to that kingdom, even here, even now.

October 22, 1997

Reflection / Discussion Questions

1. Do you have any multiracial friendships, in your congregation, your place of work, or your recreational activities? If so, how do they contribute to your understanding of each other's social situations?
2. "Racism is sinful"—not just a social problem. Why is it important to identify racism as sinful, and how do you think it grieves our Lord?
3. Do you agree that the superficiality of "buddy" movies masks the deeper issues of systematic or institutional racism? Why or why not? Can you recognize any such deep, unspoken racism in the communities in which you live?
4. The apostle Paul dealt with racial and ethnic tensions in his churches in the form of Jewish-Gentile conflicts. Our union in Christ transcends our ethnic differences, he insisted. Read Paul's Epistle to the Galatians or the Romans (especially chapters 1–3) and reflect on or discuss what you learn about the power of Christ for overcoming racism. Are there any practical implications for the life of your community? If so, explain.

PART 3

LIFE-GIVING VIRTUES

19

LIVING INTO OUR HISTORIES

O NCE UPON A TIME, there was a woman who discovered she had turned into the wrong person." So Anne
Tyler begins her latest novel, *Back When We Were
Grownups*. The woman is 53-year-old Rebecca Davitch, a
grandmother who, at least on the surface, is outgoing, joyous and "the life of the party." But Rebecca is beginning to
ask herself whether she is an impostor in her own life. Is she
living her own life? Or is it someone else's?

How do you cope with the tensions between how you
imagined your life might turn out, and how it in fact does?
Perhaps you have met significant oppression or unexpected
tragedy. Perhaps your life has brought material success but
personal emptiness. In middle age, can one find a way to
reclaim the luster of an optimistic youthfulness?

In many ways, Davitch's middle-class questioning makes
her the mirror image of the Delia Grinstead in an earlier
Tyler novel, *Ladder of Years*. Forty-year-old Delia is acutely
aware that she is living her own life, but it is one she dis-
dains. While on vacation at the beach with her physician
husband and three almost-grown children, Delia suddenly
decides to keep walking down the beach until, eventually,
she settles in a strange new town and invents a new life.

Delia wants to become an impostor in her own life, a free-
spirited and unencumbered "Ms. Grinstead" with no
responsibilities, no past, no relationships. She wants to

escape her present life and likes the thought of "beginning again from scratch." She wants to try living someone else's life, or perhaps living as if she has no life at all.

One reviewer described *Ladder of Years* as "everyone's secret fantasy." Perhaps we all imagine that there might be a way to flee our past and find a world where we can live without any burdens. Whether it is an idyllic small town, a luxurious beautiful island, a mountain retreat or a bustling anonymous city, we like to imagine a world that will offer us unmitigated happiness and give us unconstrained power to determine our own days.

But rarely does anyone actually live out that fantasy. Is it because we lack the courage to try? Or is it because we have a lurking awareness that if our fantasy were to become reality, it would begin to assume its own encumbrances and histories? Do we know that, even though we might try, we cannot escape our present life, our past and the persons we have—for better and worse—become?

Rebecca Davitch and Delia Grinstead present contrasting ways of trying to escape their present lives. One woman concludes that she has been an impostor in her own life, and so needs to assume a different character; the other wants to assume a different character by becoming an impostor.

Yet neither succeeds. Nor should we expect to succeed if we try to walk around rather than through our relationships, our encumbrances and our histories. Character cannot be invented simply by will or fantasy. It is formed over time.

A few days ago my wife and I were at a wedding. As I listened to the two people eagerly make lifelong vows to one another, I also noted the preacher's words to them, "By the grace of God, you will grow old together." It was a joyous occasion.

But what will happen to the couple as they begin to grow old together? Will they accumulate histories of grievance and bitterness, boredom and routine, encumbrances that will lead them to fear that they have become the wrong persons?

Or that they need to leave and try to begin again from scratch?

Or are there resources within the Christian tradition, including practices related to marriage, that might help prepare them for the inevitable reality that life will not turn out the way they imagine?

Could it be that our willingness to anticipate lifelong commitments will inevitably be challenged by the ways that "better or worse," "richer or poorer" and "sickness and health" turn out? Can we live into our histories even if life turns out to kill the dreams we have dreamed? Can we find ways to accept what we do and what happens to us in life's joys and griefs, successes and failures, and even its routines and boredom?

Perhaps Tyler's characters struggle with such questions because they lack the habits or practices of forgiveness and repentance. Although it is difficult to receive and offer forgiveness and repentance, these acts are central to relationships. They are also critical to learning to accept the past without being bound by it.

Forgiveness does not undo or deny the past; it offers the opportunity to redeem it. The discovery of repentance as a gift linked to forgiveness is crucial so that we can learn, over time, how to cast off those things we have done and had done to us. Repentance and forgiveness give us a daily opportunity to accept the truth of who we have become without binding us to it forever. By God's grace, the past can be redeemed and our character can be shaped in renewed ways. As a result, a forgiven and forgiving people need not try to escape the present.

As I sat in that wedding service, I wondered whether—or when—either member of this newly married couple would develop a fear that he or she had become the wrong person, or entertain a fantasy of walking away and trying to start again from scratch. But I also wondered whether their Christian convictions and practices might school them into recognizing that, although they cannot flee the past or escape the present, forgiveness and repentance might enable them to grow old together, truly by the grace of God.

July 4–11, 2001

Reflection / Discussion Questions

1. Have you ever felt like Rebecca Davitch—outwardly happy, perhaps, but on the inside, feeling something like an impostor in your own life? Could you ever have imagined years ago what your life would be like now? Explain.

2. "No man is an island," wrote John Donne centuries ago, reflecting on the deep ways in which our very identities are shaped by our relatedness to the people around us. How does this insight shape our understanding of the story of Ms. Grinstead, who tries to invent a new life for herself, one with "no responsibilities, no past, no relationships"?

3. It sounds very appealing to erase the past and begin with a completely blank slate, but the reading suggests that repentance and redemption are more realistic and more faithful ways to relate to the past than is forgetfulness. Consider and discuss how *past* is related to *present* in the stories of biblical characters such as Peter, Paul, or the woman Jesus meets at the well in John 4:1-42.

20

FIDELITY MAKES YOU HAPPY

W HAT BILL CLINTON and others like him don't understand is that sexual escapades always bring more trouble than they are worth. It is fidelity that makes you happy," my friend said. The conversation had been moving along at a rapid clip until that last sentence. Fidelity makes you happy. I hesitantly nodded in agreement. But I didn't know what to say.

I don't know if I was called up short by the audacity of that statement, a countercultural observation in the midst of our sex-obsessed culture, or by the fact that the friend who spoke is divorced, and so one who has had to struggle with failure in marriage.

Or perhaps it was because we are used to talking about these issues in terms of their negative restrictions: thou shalt not commit adultery; thou shalt not lust after another; thou shalt not have eyes for anyone other than thine own spouse. Or, as one young man commented to me about his impending marriage, "My fiancée has reminded me that once I step to the altar, I will never again sleep with another woman. Whoa."

My friend was not suggesting, of course, that sexual fidelity will make you happy in the consumer-driven sense of short-term gratification. Indeed, the desire for short-term gratification often drives sexual promiscuity.

Rather, my friend was suggesting that for those not called

to celibacy, sexual fidelity is crucial to a flourishing life. If you want to be fulfilled in life, learn how to be faithful—especially in sexual matters. It takes time, and hard work, to be faithful. Yet we discover the grace of God's love in such patient, disciplined work.

I was delighted to see these claims affirmed and eloquently amplified in Catherine M. Wallace's recent book *For Fidelity: How Intimacy and Commitment Enrich Our Lives*. Wallace began reflecting on these issues because she wanted to figure out how she would talk to her children about sex. A child of the sexual revolution, she was wary of "traditional" presumptions about sex. Yet she had concluded through her own marriage and reflections on the lives of her friends that sexual fidelity is crucial, and that such fidelity is as important for homosexual as for heterosexual relationships.

According to Wallace, sexual fidelity is a good in itself, not simply because it is useful to other ends (by preventing disease and sustaining social orders that depend on coherent family structures, for example) or because it follows from other virtues (such as justice and obedience to God). Rather, "sexual fidelity is a practice *intrinsic* to the happiness of a happy marriage." It enables us to live more flourishing lives.

Yet Wallace notes that sexual fidelity is a practice. Like other practices, such as learning to play the flute well, sexual fidelity requires discipline, effort and commitment. It requires the development of good habits.

Sexual fidelity releases us, Wallace suggests, from the consumerist self-absorption that undermines community and destroys our lives. She observes that sexual fidelity helps us understand how it is that we find ourselves precisely by losing our obsessive concern with ourselves. Put even more strongly, she believes that the practice of sexual fidelity blesses our lives and schools us for a love of, and desire for, God:

> The blessing of sexual fidelity is not a thing or a place that you reach or fail to reach. It's not a test or a task at which

you succeed or fail. Those are the wrong categories; those oppositions are category mistakes. The blessing of sexual fidelity is a process. It is a discipline or a craft or an entire way of life. It is a spiritual practice grounded in the ultimate energies of erotic desire.

It is almost as striking to think of sexual fidelity as a spiritual practice as it is to think of it as intrinsic to a flourishing life. But if, as Jews and Christians believe, we are created by God out of loving communion and for the sake of loving communion, then it should not surprise us that we would find fulfillment through fidelity. Yet, in the midst of a world in which we diminish one another and ourselves as the result of sin, we must acknowledge just how difficult—and how vulnerable—such a practice of sexual fidelity will be. We must learn and relearn how to be faithful. That is one reason why sexual promiscuity, even during our youthful exploration, is so dangerous. Habits are very difficult to break.

Sexual fidelity is vulnerable also because it requires two partners. A person committed to the practice of sexual fidelity can be severely hurt by the infidelity, the violence, the emotional abuse or even the loveless indifference of the partner. The virtue of sexual fidelity should *not* be understood as an expectation to stay within a relationship regardless of the consequences.

Our public discourses within the churches as well as in the wider culture have been corroded by our unwillingness to articulate the blessings of sexual fidelity, and the artistic discipline its practice requires throughout a lifetime. Rather than only telling our kids to "just say no," perhaps we can learn to describe for them how and why sexual fidelity enables a flourishing life.

I read Wallace's book while on vacation at the beach. As I sat on the porch overlooking the ocean one evening I saw a large ship, known colloquially as "the booze cruise," heading out for a six-hour party. Undoubtedly many of the people were simply out for a fun evening, often with their spouses. However, the ship is also notorious as a great "pick-up" spot. Indeed, a popular T-shirt there says, "I'm horny, you're drunk—how about it?"

These folks were seeking happiness. Many would wake the next morning wondering what had happened. Could it be that the claim that "the practice of sexual fidelity makes you happy" offers a prophetic witness to our culture, to our kids, and to us?

September 9–16, 1998

Reflection / Discussion Questions

1. What is it about fidelity that produces long-term happiness?
2. Sexual promiscuity is driven by the desire for short-term gratification. Why do you think so many of us seek short-term and selfish gratification at the expense of long-term and mutual happiness?
3. The story of David's adultery with Bathsheba is told in 2 Samuel 11. Read that chapter and reflect on / discuss the complicated ramifications that affected many more people than just David and Bathsheba.
4. Sexual fidelity is a discipline that involves more than just sexual intercourse; it is a way of life, a way of thinking, and a way of relating to other people. How can you shape your practical habits and patterns of thought in ways that honor the God who has given us the gift of faithful relationships? The patterns of thought that shape our lives are themselves deeply shaped by the cultures and communities in which we live. How can your congregation help nurture and shape patterns of thought and life that are contrasts to the promiscuity so deeply ingrained in our secular culture?

21

OUR CHILDREN'S HAPPINESS

I JUST WANT my child to be happy." Parents say this so often that it has become an accepted explanation for why a child is doing something other than what the parents would have hoped. And, in one sense, it seems straightforward, particularly when we consider the alternative. Do we want our children to be unhappy? Depressed? Discouraged?

Perhaps, however, the mantra has simply become a distortion that masks what we really ought to want for our children. Why should the alternative be cast in terms of happiness or unhappiness, especially in an era when we have made the pursuit of happiness such a shallow and commercial enterprise?

What if we expected parents to say, "I just want my child to be faithful"? How might that shift our expectations of parenting and of what we hope for from our children?

These questions were driven home to me in recent months by two separate yet closely related events. The first occurred at our house one Saturday. The mother of some of our kids' friends had stopped by, and in conversation she explained her generally permissive attitude toward her children's behavior by saying, "I just want my kids to be happy."

I found the phrase particularly jarring, for earlier that day I had been reading one of Origen's homilies on Abraham's call to sacrifice Isaac in Genesis 22. Origen wrote: "Who of you, do you suppose, will sometime hear the voice of an angel saying: 'Now I know that you fear God, because you spared not your son,' or your daughter or wife, or you spared not your money or the honors of the world or the ambitions of the world, but you have despised all things and 'have counted all things dung that you may gain Christ,' 'you have sold all things and have given to the poor and have followed the Word of God?' Who of you, do you think, will hear a word of this kind from the angels? Meanwhile Abraham hears this voice, and it said to him: 'You spared not your beloved son because of me.' "

Clearly we can make no sense of this awesome, difficult call from God that Abraham sacrifice his own son if we live in a world in which our highest priority is that our children be happy. It would make more sense, though be no less difficult to accept, if we understood the call—and Abraham's response—in the context of a desire that our children be faithful. We may struggle with the identity and character of the God who tests us and who calls for such a radical commitment. Yet we might also understand more deeply the character of that God who spared not God's own child for the sake of us and our salvation.

We might also begin to gain a clearer sense of what we ask from our children. Children inevitably both benefit and suffer in complex ways from the character of their parents' lives. The real question is whether they suffer for causes and convictions worthy of that suffering. We rightly ought to cry out on behalf of children who suffer because of their parents' oppression or lack of resources. We rightly ought to protest when children suffer because of their parents' selfish and self-absorbed pursuits, whether of money, sex, drugs, worldly honor and ambition or even wrongheaded religiosity.

But should we not also protest when children suffer because their parents offer them nothing worth living and dying for? When children are left with hollow and shallow lives because they have not been invited, and required, to live for something more significant than themselves? When our children are left to suffer because of our lack of convictions, or corrupt convictions, rather than because of noble and faithful ones?

Such questions became particularly poignant as I reflected on a second recent event, an exchange between a seminary student and a distinguished South African church leader. In his lecture, the churchman described his and others' involvement in the struggle against apartheid, including the risks many of them had been called to take in their discipleship. The stories were as harrowing in their details as they were inspiring in their evidence of Christian commitment.

After the lecture, the student asked the leader what his children had thought of his and his wife's involvement in the struggle. How had they coped with the risks and the suffering the family endured because of the parents' commitment to justice? The leader acknowledged that it had been very difficult. He described how painful it was for him to know that his children often were the ones who received the death threats and the epithets over the phone. He described the anxiety of being away from his family for stretches of time and praying that they would be reunited again.

Yet, he observed, all four of his children now recognize the family's involvement in the struggle as a gift. Coming to this recognition required some long and painful conversations, including the leader's own request to his children that they forgive him for the times he was away. Yet, he reported, the children have commented that even amidst the pain and suffering they endured growing up, they are grateful for the witness their family bore. They see that witness as a gift, for they recognize that their parents taught them the importance of having convictions on which you would stake your life.

Those children may indeed be happy as adults. But if so, that happiness is a reflection of a deeper and more satisfying flourishing than the more superficial hopes too many of us tend to have for our children. Such happiness as they now experience will be a wonderful by-product of having learned the more important and more profound lesson of what it means to be faithful.

May 19–26, 1999

Reflection / Discussion Questions

1. As American citizens we have canonized "the pursuit of happiness" as an inalienable right. Do you think happiness can function as an end in itself? Can the pursuit of happiness ever deliver real happiness? Explain your answers.
2. What do you think the majority of us most want out of life? What do you think God most wants for us in our lives? What do you most want out of life?
3. In Philippians 1:9-11, Paul reveals his hopes for what will happen in the lives of the Philippians. While we can be confident that he would not wish trials or persecution upon them unnecessarily, what are his real priorities, and how did he think of the difficulties to be faced in life (see verses 12-14)?

22

TRUST

W E HAD JUST moved into the parsonage of the church to which my wife had been appointed when various members of the congregation started coming by to tell us "what had really happened." Of course, all the various stories of what had happened did not cohere.

All we knew for sure was that there had been a meeting of the administrative council during which the members split into two rival groups that began meeting in separate rooms. Each group thought it was meeting as the "real" council. When the two groups came back together, a shouting match ensued, after which people threw chairs across the room at one another.

Several weeks after the meeting some people were still not speaking to one another. It was an ominous beginning for ministry, made more troubling by our inability fully to understand what had happened, whom we should believe and what histories in the church and the community had led to the events of that evening.

While I do not presume that there are many congregations in which people literally throw chairs at one another, I know many for which that is an appropriate metaphor. The fabric of trust has broken down and animosities have become entrenched. The "real" meetings are conducted not candidly in public forums but in hushed conversations in the parking lot, over the phone through the "prayer chain" or in private offices. Public meetings become either superficial exchanges of information designed to hide the animosities or—if the animosities have become exposed—verbal terrorism in which people launch mean-spirited attacks from entrenched positions.

How do we begin to move our lives and our congregations from mistrust and animosity—often entrenched in habits of many years—to the activity of reconciling discernment? Obviously, it takes patience. But it also takes corporate conversion to the one who promises to bring healing and new life even out of the most severe forms of human brokenness. Such conversion involves learning the linguistic skills and imagination necessary to begin the slow, often painful process of linking truthful speech and discernment to a trust in the fabric of the common life. Such a process takes time and is accomplished through many small gestures, decisions and actions.

In addition to the small gestures, some larger liturgical actions can serve to reorient our imagination and reshape our assumptions. My wife and I discovered a powerful example of this in a series of worship services at a United Methodist annual conference we visited as guest speakers. The conference was beset by many divisions, and so the planning committee designed the worship services to move from a confession of brokenness through forgiveness and reconciliation to a renewed sense of mission.

As we gathered the first evening a potter was on the stage, putting the final touches on a beautiful vase. As the service began, the room darkened and a spotlight appeared off to the side, where a teenager tossed a brick through a stained glass window. Even as the effects of shattered glass tingled in our ears, the spotlight turned to the potter who smashed the vase back into a lump of clay. We then began the service by confessing our brokenness. We were each handed a piece of broken glass and told to carry it with us as we contemplated our role in the brokenness of that community and of the world.

During that evening's service, the potter began the slow and laborious process of beginning—again—to craft a beautiful vase out of the clay. I could not take my eyes off him, reflecting on how much more quickly he destroyed the vase than he could restore it. So also it is with the fabric of trust in a community. A few harsh words, a malicious action, a desire to prop up my own power . . . what had I done to destroy trust, to exacerbate brokenness?

The next night we gathered again for worship. After a litany of confession, youth passed around large baskets into which we placed our pieces of broken glass. The youth took those baskets to the altar, where they dumped the pieces into a large metal tub. Over and over we heard the sounds of the shattered glass in that tub. As the last basket was emptied, a black cloth above the altar was removed, and there hung a cross made of broken glass. We then recited a litany of thanksgiving and pledged to be ambassadors of reconciliation.

Healing the brokenness in our lives and in our world takes time. Even at the end of that first service, after an hour and a half, the potter had not come close to restoring the vase he had destroyed in a fraction of a second. So also God's Holy Spirit works slowly, patiently, to make all things new in the wake of human sin and evil.

I have often wondered what would have happened had we conducted such services in the chair-throwing congregation. There is no doubt that a few services alone would not begin to accomplish the difficult work of forging trust in one another and building a faithful common life. Yet I am told that the services at the annual conference did begin to move people toward being more careful about what they said to one another and how they said it.

So I wonder: might these liturgies have helped to reshape our imaginations, to begin a process of conversion? Would we perhaps have begun to learn to disagree without being disagreeable, to trust in the God who seeks to shape among us a faithful common life? Might we have discovered that we all need to be converted, to repent of the sin of trying to control a community's life and to learn to trust one another in seeking to discern what God is calling all of us to be and to do? It is worth a try, even before the chair-throwing begins.

December 24–31, 1997

Reflection / Discussion Questions

1. Whom do you trust, and why?
2. Discuss the images from the liturgy of reconciliation described in the reading. What do they mean to you? What meaning is borne in the liturgies of your congregation's public worship?
3. The Bible represents God as a potter in numerous passages; read Jeremiah 18:1-10 and Isaiah 45:9 for two examples. God is our Creator, who is always able to reform us and our communities. What kind of re-forming is God likely working on in and among you? How can you work to embrace and not oppose this re-forming?

23

TRUTH AND LIES

W E HAD BEEN discussing *The Enchiridion on Faith, Hope, and Love,* Augustine's brief exposition of the essential teachings of Christianity. One of the students was perplexed by the fact that in discussing evil Augustine used the example of lying.

Why, I wondered aloud to the class, would Augustine turn to lying? After all, he had written in other books about profound social evils and horrifying examples of injustice and suffering.

Another student said Augustine is surely wrong in stating that "it seems certain that every lie is a sin." The student cited a story that serves as one of modernity's favorite justifications for lying: What if you were in Nazi Germany and you were sheltering Jews in your home. The Nazis come to the door and ask if you are sheltering Jews. Should you lie or tell the truth?

The students began reflecting on what Augustine might say in response to that question. One student found it difficult to imagine that Augustine would be so hard-hearted as to insist on not lying over showing compassion to protect the Jews. Another student suggested that we get too uptight about "personal" morality like lying, when the really crucial issues have to do with systemic injustice.

Eventually, one of the quieter students in the class intervened. She asked, "Could it be that the problem is less in the questions than in ourselves? We like to talk about sheltering Jews from the Nazis, because we see ourselves as basically good people who occasionally tell lies for good—or at least harmless—reasons. But that really lets us off the hook too easily. Most of us find it all too easy to lie, and we don't even tend to notice how destructive our lying becomes."

Her comment was followed by a rather stunned silence. She was clearly on to something that had less to do with Augustine's argument than with our own lives. Or, better, she had suggested why Augustine's example of lying seemed to speak so clearly to our own lives.

I rephrased her insight: If we are basically truthful people, then we can afford to justify lying in the service of noble causes. Augustine's point, however, seems to challenge the fundamental premise: we are, he suggests, people who find it all too easy to lie.

This clearly made us uncomfortable. I offered a challenge: Would our entire class, professor included, agree that for one full week we would do our best not to tell a single lie to ourselves or anyone else? This would *not* mean that we would say every true thing we thought, I said, since being truthful can be used in destructive ways. Following this rule would likely mean that all of us would have to be quiet much more often as we discovered situations and relationships in which it is better not to speak than to utter statements that are not true.

None of us—myself included—was particularly interested in accepting the challenge. We thought it would require too much effort. One student noted, "It would also require us to begin rethinking the assumptions we make about our society and our relationships." That seemed more than any of us was ready to tackle.

Over the past few weeks I have thought a lot about that extraordinary class discussion. We have a president [Clinton] who has apparently found it easy to lie and be deceptive about his relationships with women. We have Monica Lewinsky on a tape-recorded conversation saying that lying is not difficult: "I've done it all my life." We have the independent counsel's office reportedly leaking stories about confidential testimony before the grand jury.

Does it really matter? Is lying primarily a matter of "personal" morality separable from larger social issues? Did Augustine overstate his case, both about the prevalence of lying in our lives and about its importance in discussions of good and evil?

Or could it be that we have become so used to lying that we now find it difficult to tell the truth? Do we know what it means to discern the truth in other people's comments? Do we have the courage to speak the truth, even when it is not to our advantage? Can we *do* the truth if we do not even know how to recognize it?

Within our churches, do we know what it means to speak the truth to one another, much less to do it in love? Or do we rest content with backstabbing gossip and passive-aggressive avoidance?

I have been impressed by the courageous and profoundly hopeful work of South Africa's Truth and Reconciliation Commission. The people of South Africa have committed themselves to learning to speak the truth to one another and to do so in a spirit not of vengeance but of reconciliation. It is a daring experiment, a ray of hope that testifies that the darkness has not overcome us.

The commission understands Augustine's point about the corrosive effects of lies and deceptions, particularly when they have been put in the service of such profound injustice. But it also understands the gospel's convictions that we are capable of learning to tell the truth—understood both as discernment and as speech—in the context of a struggle for reconciliation.

Perhaps we need many more truth and reconciliation commissions—for our political culture in Washington, D.C., for the churches, for our classrooms, and perhaps for many other arenas. Does the gospel ask of us anything less?

March 11, 1998

Reflection / Discussion Questions

1. When was the last time you told a lie? Include not only bald-faced lies, but also your attempts to avoid telling the truth.
2. What do you think makes lying so destructive?
3. What do you think of the diagnosis that we are not good people who occasionally lie for noble ends, but that we are people all too ready to lie and deceive in instances where it might be advantageous and where the chances of our getting caught seem slim?
4. In the Gospel of John, Jesus identifies himself as "the way, and the *truth*, and the life" (14:6, emphasis added). Discuss what it means that Jesus calls himself "the truth." Find instances of words such as *true* or *truth* in John to help you. What is the opposite of truth in this case?

24

HALLOWTHANKSMAS

We ARE COMING to the close of the season of HallowThanksMas. It begins the last week of October and extends until Christmas Day. At the end of October the children are loaded up on sugar that doesn't seem to leave their systems until early January. Shopping centers have Christmas decorations up in mid-October, and then the materialistic press to buy more and more sets in. Throughout this season, adults become frenetic, anxious and—all too often—depressed. Such depression is particularly acute for those people whose calendars are not filled and who feel more acutely than ever the absence of places to go, of loved ones with whom to celebrate.

I have never liked HallowThanksMas. In the past, I went along with a grudging acceptance that it was something we—and particularly those of us with children—just had to endure. I have found ways to resist the excessive sugar and the materialism of the season. This year, however, I reflected on the ways in which the frenetic pace of HallowThanksMas may be a microcosm of our culture throughout the year—including especially my own life.

It was late in October, the weekend before the beginning of HallowThanksMas. I was getting ready to fly out to the Midwest for a retreat I was leading for clergy and laity. The folks had requested that I reflect on the theme "Connecting to Our Calling." I thought I would spend a portion of the time reflecting on the ways in which, though our lives are filled with things to do, we often find ourselves unfulfilled. I would propose the Christian practice of "keeping sabbath" as a way to find renewal in our own calling as disciples and ministers of the gospel.

Just before I got on the plane, I bought a copy of James Gleick's new book *Faster: The Acceleration of Just About Everything*. I thought it might provide some helpful background. I mused about multiple ironies: that I was reading a book about the acceleration of just about everything on an airplane whose arrival was very close to the beginning of the retreat because I had needed to attend several meetings earlier in the morning. And I was reading the book because I still needed to prepare some final details for the retreat because I just hadn't had enough time to work on it earlier in the week.

I finally put down Gleick's book, not finding it as helpful as I had hoped. Instead I began reading Dorothy Bass's *Receiving the Day: Christian Practices for Opening the Gift of Time*. Though I was confident that this book would be illuminating and enjoyable, I had been hesitant to open it partly because I had already shaped my comments about "keeping sabbath" for the retreat, and so reading it seemed less urgent, and partly because I sensed that I might need to change some habits of work and scheduling if I took her argument seriously.

On page three Bass's gracious words hit me square between the eyes: "Busy people may think that what we need is a few more open boxes on the pages of our datebooks." Yes! I thought. "But in fact that would provide only a flat and short-lived remedy, and not only because those boxes would soon fill up like all the others. What we really need is time of a different quality. We need the kind of time that is measured in a yearly round of feasts and fasts, in a life span that begins when a newborn is placed in her parents' arms, and in a day that ends and begins anew as a line of darkness creeps across the edge of the earth. This kind of time exists, but we have learned not to notice it. Our gaze is fixed instead on a datebook, some of us anxiously hoping to squeeze into its little boxes all that we must do, others weeping to see that so many of the pages are blank." Oh.

I discovered that what I most needed, and what our culture most needs, is not a sharp disjunction between faster and slower, or even the rhythms of six days of work and a day of rest. Nor do we even need simply the fuller understanding of sabbath as a time both for rest and for family and community. Rather, we need "time of a different quality."

As I read *Receiving the Day* I felt the force of God's judgment. Yet as is the case with genuinely receiving God's judgment, I sensed a judgment of grace. Instead of trying to cram time for sabbath-keeping into my schedule, or even adding "rest" at the end of my "to do" list, I discovered a need and a desire to cultivate practices for "opening the gift of time." Could I refocus my life in a way that keeps the gospel's sense of time at the heart of my life, in the core of my imagination? Can we refocus our lives in such a way?

As I have lived through the last two months, I have realized that I am not disturbed by the busyness of HallowThanksMas. I enjoy being busy. But I am disturbed by the frenetic pace that lacks the quality of time that renews, refreshes and redeems. This year, though my schedule is still full and there are few empty boxes, I have sought to resist HallowThanksMas more intentionally. By contrast, Advent—one of the central ways in which Christians open the gift of time—has become again for me a time of patience, of preparation, of repentance. This year, I think I will be ready for Christmas.

December 22–29, 1999

Reflection / Discussion Questions

1. What is the season of HallowThanksMas like for you? Is it a frenetic blur from which you recover sometime in mid-January or perhaps a difficult reminder of loneliness or the losses of past holiday seasons? Explain.

2. Have you ever tried to keep a sabbath day, to establish a cycle of work balanced by a day of worship and rest? Christians are not bound by the ceremonial laws of the sabbath, but many Christians have found they feel healthier and even that they are more productive by taking a sabbath day. What might a Christian practice of sabbath-keeping mean for you?

3. Romans 5:6 says that Christ came and died for us "at just the right time" (NIV). Jesus told his disciples that the time of his return was imminent but unknown to everyone but the Father (Matthew 24:36). How can we live in this "time between the times" in a way that values the present time won for us by Christ's redemption and looks forward to that great and glorious time when time shall be no more?

25

ANSWERIZING

A PASTOR CALLS the kids to the altar rail for yet another children's sermon and says: "I am thinking of something that is brown, has a bushy tail, and every fall gathers acorns to itself. What am I thinking of?" After a long silence, a young child pipes up: "I'm sure the right answer is Jesus, but it sure sounds like a squirrel to me."

This joke has made the rounds among preachers as a mocking critique of the triviality of many children's sermons. It can also serve to illustrate a tendency that is polarizing people and crippling our capacity for meaningful discourse: the belief that we know what the right answer is, regardless of the question that has been asked or the issue being addressed.

David James Duncan, the author of *The Brothers K*, characterizes this attitude as "answerizing." It grows out of the conviction that the only right way to handle any question is to offer The One Correct Answer. In a lecture titled, "Who Owns the West? Ten Wrong Answers," Duncan describes answerizing as "an activity that stands in relationship to truly Answering as the ability to memorize the phone book stands in relationship to the ability to love every preposterous flesh and blood person whose mere name the phone book happens to contain."

Duncan goes on to note: "Questions that tap into our mortality, our pain, our selfishness, our basic needs, questions that arise from the immeasurable darkness, lightness or mystery of our lives, require more than mere Answerization." Such questions require sustained conversation, a willingness to listen and speak with one another in ways that can acknowledge the complexity of our lives; Christians believe such complexity involves the God whom we worship.

Job's friends were experts at answerizing. They were unable to tolerate the inexplicable complexity and mystery of Job's suffering and were sure there must obviously be One Correct Answer to his predicament. Job refuses their answers by insisting that his suffering remains a mystery. We know with whom God sides in that story.

Yet we have not absorbed God's critique of Job's friends or of our attempts to answerize. So we encounter fundamentalists on the ecclesial right and left. On one side people are convinced that the right answer is Jesus, even if the question sounds like the answer ought to be a squirrel. On the other side, people are convinced that the right answer is an "ism," or an appeal to privileged personal experience, regardless of whether the question or issue can be so neatly explained.

Answerizing also has become the dominant mode of political discourse. Tune into the Sunday morning talk shows and watch the politicians and "spin doctors" utter their predetermined statements regardless of the question that is actually asked.

These tendencies toward answerizing are threatening to debase our conversations and our communities. Rather than being reduced to verbal trench warfare, can we find common ground? Can we find ways of recognizing that we are sharply divided about deeply held beliefs, but do so in ways that nonetheless sustain us at a level deeper than a thin veneer of tolerance masking hostility?

Perhaps we ought to search for meaningful disagreements with one another. If we develop and articulate our convictions as clearly and coherently as possible, we will likely discover profound and potentially alienating disagreements among our friends, strangers and enemies. But if we patiently develop skills of attending and listening to others in all of their "preposterous flesh and blood" particularity, then those disagreements will more likely be meaningful. Communities are sustained both by painfully won consensus and by an ability to work through—and to live with—meaningful disagreements.

How do we discover common ground and sustain ourselves through meaningful disagreements? As Mark Schwehn has suggested in *Exiles from Eden,* three virtues are particularly important: humility, truthfulness and interpretive charity. Humility emphasizes that "we see but through a glass darkly." In some contexts, it is important to affirm that we do see, that we must make and defend claims to knowledge and truth. But it is also important to recognize what we do not know, and to recognize that we need others to deepen the mystery of our engagement with the world, particular objects of study, and God.

A commitment to truth and to truthfulness changes the horizons of inquiry, conversation and debate. No longer are opposing sides seeking victory through rhetorical giftedness or deployments of power. Rather, people are engaged in a joint inquiry in which we are required to listen to, and learn from, one another. This joint inquiry may involve polemics and apologetics. However, it also leaves open the distinct possibility of intellectual conversion—of being persuaded by the other's views.

Interpretive charity requires us to interpret the other's views in the best light possible. Rather than having a predetermined One Correct Answer for our interlocutor, we are called to listen to the other in ways that open our minds to deeper understanding. Interpretive charity invites a hermeneutic of generosity, whether in our engagement with texts such as scripture or with particular people.

In the place of answerizing, we need to cultivate qualities

of life that enable us faithfully to address those questions that "tap into our mortality, our pain, our selfishness, our basic needs, questions that arise from the immeasurable darkness, lightness, or mystery of our lives." Such questions, I would add, tap into our faithful worship of the triune God whose power is manifested in the powerlessness of the cross, whose wisdom is foolishness to the Greeks, whose kingdom we see but through a glass darkly.

November 18–25, 1998

Reflection / Discussion Questions

1. Can you think of any patterns of answerizing in your own conversations? Do you recognize it in other people when you are conversing with them? In what ways? Tune into some talk radio or other news programs today and listen for such patterns. What complicated problems in our society seem to get nothing but "answerized" responses?

2. Are there any issues or questions in the life of your congregation that seem to be going nowhere because the disease of answerizing has infected your ability to discuss them? If so, briefly outline or describe some. Prioritizing the commitment to listen and the commitment to a shared Christian solution over one's commitment to winning the argument is a key step in overcoming answerizing.

3. How do Christian virtues such as humility, truthfulness, interpretive charity, and patience help us become people of discernment rather than answerizers?

4. Set aside some time and read through the Book of Job, following the cycles of answerizing speeches given by Job's "friends." How would you characterize their interactions? What lessons can be learned from them?

26

IMAGINING SCRIPTURE

IT SEEMS TO ME a wonderful irony that Christians in America are preoccupied with debates about biblical authority just when all parties to the debates are less knowledgeable about the content of scripture than many of our predecessors were. On college campuses, teachers of English literature find it difficult to teach texts like *Paradise Lost*, *Moby Dick* or Toni Morrison's *Beloved* because students are unable to grasp the biblical allusions. In churches, preachers comment on the lack of biblical literacy among their parishioners, and the pastors' comments sometimes deflect attention from their own illiteracy.

This lack of familiarity with scripture weakens our capacity for theological reflection, moral discernment and spiritual nurture. It also impoverishes our vocabulary for characterizing God, the world and the purpose and destiny of our lives.

Yet, troubling as biblical illiteracy may be, I am even more troubled by our lack of imagination and sophistication in interpreting the whole story of scripture. As my colleague David Steinmetz said, "We are better readers of detective fiction than we are of scripture." He noted that reading scripture well is a lot like reading detective fiction—what you discover later in the story equips you to see the earlier parts with fresh and illuminating eyes.

Steinmetz understands these connections because he has

devoted much of his career to interpreting our forebears' interpretations of scripture. He has discovered a sophisticated, imaginative conversation that is more like contemporary approaches to detective fiction or other novels than what we have come to call "exegesis."

Could it be that we know less of the content of scripture because we have made it so boring? We flatten scripture when we read the text only for what lies behind it, or in segments or as a collection of guidelines for moral living. Who wouldn't rather reread *Beloved* than study a series of texts that we cannot connect to a larger narrative, much less to our convictions about the Triune God whom we worship?

I am not saying that we should ignore the gains in understanding that have been achieved by the "higher criticism" of the past two centuries. We need the best philological and historical methods we can develop. But we also need to learn how to read imaginatively, how to move back and forth both intratextually and intertextually.

This became clear to me in reading Gary Anderson's book *The Genesis of Perfection: Adam and Eve in Jewish and Christian Imagination*. Anderson takes on those vexing opening chapters of the Bible, Genesis 1–3. But he does so by exploring how the modern debates have been received by interpreters in both Jewish and Christian thought.

The book is a sheer delight. It has altered my thinking about how best to interpret the story of Adam and Eve, and it extends an invitation to scripture that is far more engaging, imaginative and theologically illuminating than what we hear in most synagogues or churches. Anderson makes the story come alive, both in its particulars and in its larger implications.

He takes us on an elegant journey that includes the rest of scripture, patterns of interpretation by rabbis and Christian theologians in the early postbiblical era, the art of Michelangelo and the fiction of John Milton. The continual retelling of the Adam and Eve story, he explains, illumines, challenges and transforms "conventional" understandings of its original context. He also shows how liturgical settings, artistic renderings and scholarly commentary are typically interwoven in a rich and complicated conversation.

Anderson's invitation to that conversation encourages us to become sophisticated and imaginative readers. He writes:

> The story of Adam and Eve is very, very short. The story of Joseph and his brothers is easily ten times as long if not longer. Yet the very brevity of the [Adam and Eve] tale, along with the knotty questions it leaves unanswered, cries out for some sort of interpretive expansion. Jewish and Christian readers set about to fill in these gaps by correlating them to other parts of the biblical story. Like readers returning to the opening pages of a novel, they reread—and eventually rewrote—the story of human beginnings in light of where they believed them to point.

How can we learn to weave together the insights of philological and historical investigation—exegesis—with the imaginative readings of our forebears? I took a first step by participating in seminars sponsored by the Center of Theological Inquiry. A group of 15 people made up of biblical scholars, historical theologians, systematic theologians and pastors gathered to read scripture together. Steinmetz noted that, collectively, we represented the skills a single interpreter would have been expected to have in earlier eras.

It took us a while to stop protecting the turf of our disciplines. But once we did, we began to see connections—and to discover interpretive partners both ancient and contemporary—that made reading scripture more imaginative, more fun and more theologically significant than it had been before. As a result, I have learned more about the content of scripture and become more supple in my judgments about its authority. Best of all, I've learned that there is a rich reservoir of ancient and contemporary conversation partners who can aid us all in the art of reading, interpreting and imagining scripture.

June 19–26, 2002

Reflection / Discussion Questions

1. What are your favorite stories in Scripture? Why do you find them so engaging?
2. Discuss with other Christians what the storyline of the Bible is like. What are its basic movements from Genesis through the end of the New Testament?
3. David Steinmetz noted that the Bible is like detective fiction in that what you learn later in the story sheds light on what happens earlier. Read a few passages such as Matthew 2:6 and 2:15, and their Old Testament counterparts in Micah 5:2 and Hosea 11:1. How do you think the life, death, and resurrection of Jesus inspired Matthew to tell the story of Jesus in light of the Old Testament?
4. How can imaginative reading of scripture help us to cultivate the virtue of wisdom—wisdom that we need to guide us in Christian life?

PART 4

FACING
CHALLENGES

27

CHECKBOOK REVELATIONS

WOULD YOU COME and lead a series of classes on sexuality, drawing particularly on our denomination's statement on sexuality?" Such was the request from the leader of a congregation's adult Sunday school class. Even though I normally am predisposed to accept such invitations, it did not take me long to decline this one.

I said that in our cultural and ecclesial climate, sexuality is a topic almost guaranteed to generate heat without providing light. I suggested that most congregations, including theirs, needed first to learn how to discuss less divisive issues. If members could develop habits of sustaining a community of discernment over less controversial concerns, then perhaps they would be equipped to grapple with the more explosive issues.

The leaders seemed intrigued by my suggestion, and we agreed that I would do a series on cultivating a community of discernment. The first session focused on a rather curious passage in Ephesians (4:25–5:1). Stephen Fowl at Loyola College titled a reflection on this passage, "How to Make Stealing Possible." He noticed that, in the midst of a passage which seems to focus on how people talk with one another, there is an injunction that "those who are stealing should give up stealing." What could that mean? Is it simply an odd interpolation? After all, the passage reads well, and perhaps even better, if the verse is removed. Or does the verse fit within the larger context of the passage and of the letter as a whole?

In Fowl's view, the key is found in the passage's framing reference: "We are members of one another." When people hold things in common, the risk of stealing becomes greater—for there is a chance that some will take advantage of the others and not carry their share of the burden. Hence the verse includes an injunction that those who give up stealing should "labor and work honestly with their own hands, so as to have something to share with the needy." In Fowl's suggestive phrase, we make stealing "possible" by cultivating a common life in which we truly depend on one another. There is heightened risk, but also the heightened possibility for holy living in which all contribute to the sustenance of the common good.

I presented this perspective to the class, noting that the Ephesians passage presumes that we are sharing enough of our resources to make stealing possible. Is that true of this class, I asked. I offered a proposal: all members of the class (including me) should bring our checkbooks to class the following week so that we could compare what we are actually doing with our resources. Unsurprisingly, and with no small measure of relief on my part, my suggestion was met with a stony silence. No one wanted to take up my proposal. Why not?

In part, I think, it is because we are so accustomed to thinking that economic matters are private. We do not believe that we should be expected to reveal how much we earn, much less how we spend it. Curiously, we seem more willing to divulge information about our sexual attitudes and behaviors than our stewardship. This is certainly true in our television culture of exposure, where talk shows are filled with people disclosing bizarre sexual behavior, but where standards of compensation and stewardship are rarely subjected to scrutiny.

It is also true in the church. There seems to be an implicit agreement among many clergy and laity that, apart from the annual stewardship Sunday that is necessary in order to underwrite the budget, economic matters are personal and private in nature and are unrelated to the corporate, public life of Christians. Hence I had mentioned a taboo subject in proposing that the members of the Sunday school class show their checkbooks to one another.

Yet, ironically, Christians are at least dimly aware that the Bible—and Jesus in particular—seems far more interested in money than sex. Jesus goes so far as to say, "Where your treasure is, there will your heart be also." In another story, the rich young ruler walks away sad, because he had many possessions to which he was more attached than he was to God.

Could it be that we are afraid to open our checkbooks because we know that they reveal far more than how we spend our money? That they indeed reveal our hearts, our conflicted desires, the god(s) whom we really worship?

To be sure, if we lack a common life and exist as strangers to one another—even in our church, even in our Sunday school classes—then revealing our checkbooks to one another is probably too much as a first step. We would become vulnerable too quickly, and open ourselves to the potential of voyeurism and gossip that destroys communities and lives. Even so, first steps are desperately needed—and they need to be made from the pulpit, in our meetings, in the expectations we create for one another as "members of one another" within the church community.

During our conversations in the Sunday school class about what our checkbooks might reveal, one of the members made an interesting observation. She noted that we find it relatively easy to talk about sexuality—in particular, such issues as adultery and homosexuality—because most of us in churches do so without fear that the discussion will require us to change our lives. Yet, she observed, it is very difficult for us to talk about our own economic practices because—particularly in a relatively wealthy congregation—the discussion would likely implicate us all in a call to repentance.

Her conclusion was insightful: perhaps our lives would be deeper and richer if we began to talk with one another about matters with which all of us need to struggle, whether that struggle be with abundance or crippling poverty. For those of us who would have to be judged among the world's wealthy, money matters call us to reexamine and change our lives. After all, Jesus was interested in our money only because he was interested in our life.

February 3–10, 1999

Reflection / Discussion Questions

1. What topics are off-limits in your congregation? What would the reaction be if your pastor preached about sexuality from the pulpit? What about tithing? What about the use of our income to buy bigger houses and newer cars?

2. Do you think that the way we spend our discretionary income is a private matter? Why or why not? Is it different from other parts of our lives of public discipleship to Jesus Christ? What are the dangers here? What limits might be appropriate? Read the story of Ananias and Sapphira in Acts 5:1-10, and remember that their community was very different from ours. What lessons can we learn from their story about God's concern that our financial management be a part of our Christian discipleship?

3. Jesus said that our hearts will follow our treasure (Matthew 6:21). Think about or look through your own

checkbook or your weekly planner to see where you are investing your treasures of time and money. Where is your treasure leading your heart?

4. An eighteenth-century person once lamented that he simply could not tithe when his income was $30 per week. He literally could not survive on less than $28 per week, and $2 is not quite 10% of $30. Later in his life when he began to earn $70 per week, the valuable lesson he learned about living on $28 enabled him to give away $42. A great many American Christians are in a position more like that of the older person than when he was younger—we earn far more than we really need. What would happen if we took stock of our stewardship and considered our priorities from the perspective of discipleship to Jesus Christ?

28

WHO IS A PERSON?

TWO OF THE most powerful intellectual and social forces in our culture are the hard sciences and capitalist economics. Together they have conspired to produce images of personhood that undermine Christian understandings. According to these images, persons are defined by their rational capacities and their productive contributions. These images often lead us to dangerous judgments at the edges of life: we consider genetic testing for mental handicaps and abortion at the beginning of life, and euthanasia and physician-assisted suicide at the end.

Christianity presumes that we are creatures made in the image and likeness of God, destined for communion with God. The praise of God in Christian worship invites persons to participate regardless of their cognitive abilities or their productive usefulness.

Oliver Sacks illumines this point in his story of Jimmie G., "The Lost Mariner," in *The Man Who Mistook His Wife for a Hat*. Jimmie was a charming, intelligent and handsome 49-year-old man. Unfortunately, he had lost his memory. Puzzled by the phenomenon of an otherwise healthy man who had lost his capacity to remember, Sacks asked himself, "What sort of a life (if any), what sort of world, what sort of a self, can be preserved in a man who has lost the greater part of his memory and, with this, his past and his moorings in time?"

Jimmie was able neither to function rationally nor to contribute productively in a job. He lived his life as if he were still 19, for his memory had frozen some 30 years earlier. He could not remember events or people from day to day, or even from minute to minute. Sacks thought of Jimmie as a lost self, a lost soul, unaware of his condition because it engulfed him and the world into the vortex of a meaningless present.

Perhaps Sacks's bewilderment was as much a factor of modernity's restricted conception of personhood as anything else. Sacks concluded that since medical science was unaware of a way to help Jimmie, Jimmie was probably "beyond help." "One tended to speak of [Jimmie] instinctively as a spiritual casualty—a 'lost soul,' " said Sacks. "Was it possible that he had really been 'desouled' by a disease?"

Sacks spoke with Roman Catholic nuns who cared for Jimmie in a nursing home. "Do you think he has a soul?" The sisters were outraged by the question, but understood why Sacks asked it. "Watch Jimmie in chapel," they said, "and judge for yourself." So Sacks observed Jimmie in worship:

> I saw here an intensity and steadiness of attention and concentration that I had never seen before in him. . . . I watched him kneel and take the sacrament on his tongue, and could not doubt the fullness and totality of communion, the perfect alignment of his spirit with the spirit of the mass. Fully, intensely, quietly, in the quietude of absolute concentration and attention, he entered and partook of the holy communion.

Sacks realized that Jimmie's soul was revealed in the act of moral attention in worship, and in the aesthetic and dramatic activity of praising God. His soul was touched, held and stilled as he gave his attention to the liturgy and participated in communion. He had no difficulty in "following" music or simple dramas, "for every moment in music and art refers to, contains, other moments." He would fall apart in purely mental activities, but in worship he found a profound peace in and through emotional and spiritual attention to art, music and the mass.

Jimmie's personhood could not be circumscribed by memory, productivity or rationality. Moving beyond the limits of ordinary cognitive ability, Jimmie praised God with body and soul.

January 26, 2000

Reflection / Discussion Questions

1. Have you ever known anyone, a friend or family member, with diminished mental capacities? If so, what have you learned from him or her about human personality?
2. If rationality or the ability to contribute productively to society are insufficient measures of our personhood, what might you suggest are other, more suitable criteria for defining what it means to be a person? What lessons can we learn from the biblical teaching about creation or redemption? What distinguishes human creatures from all other parts of creation in Genesis 1?
3. How can these biblical lessons about personhood inform our complex discussions about abortion, euthanasia, physician-assisted suicide, or human cloning?
4. How do these same biblical lessons about personhood influence the way we think about and treat even "normal" adult people in the course of our everyday lives?

29

ROOTS OF VIOLENCE

JONESBORO, Paducah, Springfield. These towns have become synonymous with random youth killings in schools. Close to two dozen people have been killed in school shootings over the past two years, many more have been injured, and thousands have been emotionally scarred by the trauma.

We search for ways to explain such events. We *need* to understand these events as best we can, to try to make sense of the senseless acts that threaten our identity. We do so to honor the memory and the suffering of those who died or were injured. In addition, we do so hoping to learn some lessons that might diminish the likelihood of future Jonesboros.

We do so even though, as Christians, we recognize that explanations for sin always fall short. Loving God makes sense; turning away from God and our neighbor, and turning in on ourselves, does not. How else can we account for the fact that we continue to sin, even when we know it diminishes ourselves and others?

It is impossible fully to know how and why these events happened. But several compelling analyses have identified important contributing factors. One of the most obvious is the easy accessibility of guns in our culture, and our fascination with them. We have failed to develop sensible policies about gun control. Charlton Heston, the new president of the National Rifle Association, responded to the recent rash of school shootings with the following observation: the perpetrators "are already career criminals, or trembling on the brink." It is almost laughable to hear an 11-year-old Arkansas boy described in these terms, but Heston's comments reveal the cynicism that undermines our public discourse about guns. We seem unable to learn even the most obvious lessons.

A second factor is our culture's fascination with violence. I have no doubt that the prevalence of violence in the media significantly affects both our tendencies toward violence and our tolerance of it. I notice it in myself, and I have watched it in my own kids. It only took watching one episode of *Power Rangers* to discover that it encouraged my boys, then seven and four, to interact in much more violent ways. The recurring images of violence—on television, in movies, in music—shape our imaginations and cultivate aggressive passions that lead to our own violent outbursts.

Closely related to media violence is a third factor: imitative violence. There seems little doubt that each of the school killings has provided an opportunity for copycats. This is not to say that the motives and circumstances in each of the recent episodes were identical. Yet each successive episode seems to have been affected by the spectacle of earlier killings.

This kind of imitation goes well beyond the recent wave of shootings in schools. René Girard has suggested that mimetic violence is woven into the fabric of human culture and into each human being's earliest experiences with desire. We desire what we cannot have, and we want to have it. Our acquisitive desire leads us into violence.

My reflections on the school killings have been shaped partly by Girard's reflections and partly by my own experience as a parent. After all, my oldest child is the same age— 11—as one of the two perpetrators of the killings in Jonesboro. As I reflected on whether I could imagine my children becoming violent in this way, I worried about each of the factors described above. Yet I was also haunted by the recognition that we can never fully explain why we sin in the particular ways we do. I cannot guarantee that my children will not become violent. Yet how do we raise them so as to minimize the risk?

Girard believes that the crucified and risen Christ offers the antidote to mimetic violence. Christ refuses to be drawn into our destructive cycles of violence. Even though our violence nails Jesus to the cross, he refuses to retaliate. The risen Christ offers a judgment of grace, a judgment that does not condemn those who killed him but offers life in God's new creation. This new creation is to be embodied in communities whose practices reflect the gracious and peaceable character of God's reign.

Yet cultivating such communities requires more of Christians than many of us have wanted to acknowledge. The African proverb that "it takes a village to raise a child" is, Christianly understood, a reminder that it takes a church to raise a Christian child. But some of the most powerful forces shaping our children often appear to be antithetical to Christian discipleship.

Physically gifted kids discover a temporary satisfaction of their desires through the adulation that comes with team sports. Physically attractive kids discover a temporary satisfaction of their desires through sexual activity. Affluent kids discover a temporary satisfaction of their desires through acquiring material goods that represent the latest in status symbols. Unfortunately, but in some sense not unexpectedly, kids who do not fit in, kids who have been victims of the exclusionary tactics so typical of adolescent relations, too often turn to violence—either projected outward, in acts of aggression, or inward, through depression and suicide.

Do we teach our children what is worth living for? Dying for? Do we school them, as we ourselves need to be schooled, in imitation of the crucified and risen Christ? What practices of Christian community do we need to culti-

135

vate for youth that draws them into imitation that nurtures love for God and neighbor? Can those practices provide a sense of adventure powerful enough to counteract other forces that tempt us?

The series of youth school killings should serve as a wake-up call. I hope that, among other things, it can awaken us to the need to provide a deeper sense of Christian identity and discipleship for our kids, and for ourselves.

July 15–22, 1998

Reflection / Discussion Questions

1. In your own experience or that of your family or acquaintances, can you recognize the pattern of violence described? Do violent games or forms of entertainment shape your thoughts and your tolerance for violence?
2. In large measure it is the unpredictability of school killings that scares many of us. If you have children, how have you talked with them about these things? How can we as a culture nurture children in such a way that these kinds of incidents can be prevented in the future?
3. The reading suggests that Christ's refusal to participate in mimetic violence is the key to breaking out of our current cultural cycle. Read the story of Jesus' arrest in Matthew 26:47-56, and discuss what our Lord teaches his disciples about the use of violence. What might that mean for our day-to-day habits?

30

PSALMS OF RAGE

SHE MUST BE WRONG about saying you can get angry at God. That goes against everything I've been taught about God. That would suggest that God has done something wrong." A layperson was responding to Ellen Davis's provocative new book *Getting Involved with God: Rediscovering the Old Testament.* I had chosen the book as a focus for a seminar that draws clergy and laity together several times a year to read and discuss matters of faith and life.

Davis does a superb job of writing, as she puts it, "about getting, and staying, involved with God—what it takes, what it costs, what it looks and feels like, why anyone would want to do it anyway." We get involved with God because, as the Old Testament communicates over and over again, "God is involved with us, deeply and irrevocably so."

Davis shows how human involvement with God in the Old Testament is expressed through voices and moods that range from grief to joy, from complaint to thanksgiving, from "uncontained rage to dumbfounded gratitude." It was this last pairing that troubled the layperson, who found the notion of speaking to God in "uncontained rage" to be deeply problematic.

I asked whether his objection was to Davis's analysis or to the psalmist's expression of rage (as in Psalm 137—"Happy shall they be who take your little ones / and dash them against the rock!"). He acknowledged that although the "cursing psalms," as Davis describes them, are part of scripture, he didn't know what to do with them. He was uncomfortable with the suggestion that "these psalms are available and even appropriate for Christian prayer, and sometimes they are necessary."

Davis adds that these psalms "must be used responsibly, or they become dangerous to ourselves and to others." But my colleague was not convinced that they could be used responsibly.

He joins Christians through the centuries who have been troubled by the "cursing psalms" and have struggled to discern their compatibility with the character of the God whom we worship. Regardless of how we spin it, these prayers seem to endorse hatred and rage.

As we discussed the layperson's objections and concern, we were able to make two crucial distinctions. First, we all agreed that the language of lamenting to God—expressing great sorrow, anguish and complaint—is appropriate, and can be a life-giving way of being involved with God.

Second, we agreed that blaming God by holding God morally culpable is inappropriate. God is not at fault in how God deals with the world. Assigning blame to God, which sometimes includes the notion of a psychologically satisfying but theologically problematic act of "forgiving God," is inappropriate. It leads to distorted conceptions of God's character and engagement with the world and our lives.

We referred to the injunction in Ephesians to "be angry but do not sin" (4:26), exploring how anger might be a sign of life and a powerful protest against injustice and wickedness. Some acknowledged that some of the difficulty was due to lingering memories of parents who had enjoined them with specific instructions about appropriate piety—especially in prayer. These participants wondered if they needed to find prayerful ways of giving voice to the anger they experienced and didn't know what to do about.

Even so, we could not imagine how delight in bashing babies against the rocks could be anything but sinful. So we examined Davis's analysis more carefully. She notes that our attempts to ignore these psalms lead us to repress our own feelings of rage and bitterness in the face of betrayal, intense suffering or inexplicable injustice. "By refusing to listen to that anger and even take it on our lips, we lose an opportunity to bring our own anger into the context of our relationship with God. The cursing psalms are . . . indispensable if we are to come before God with rigorous honesty. They are necessary not only for our individual spiritual health but also for maintaining or restoring the health of the church."

Davis adds two notes. First, she emphasizes that in demanding that our enemies be driven into God's judgment, we also open them up—alas!—to God's mercy. Perhaps we have to acknowledge the temptation of Jonah to become embittered at God's character as gracious and merciful, slow to anger and abounding in steadfast love, and ready to relent from punishing. Are we ready to drive our enemies into God's hands?

Second, Davis suggests that we interpret a psalm by turning it 180 degrees. Is there anyone who might want to say this to God about me—or maybe, about us? Might we discover not only a rigorously honest engagement with our own passions of righteous indignation but also the legitimacy of others' complaints against us?

At the end of our discussion, some participants were still not persuaded by Davis's analysis or my interpretations. But in the process we had probed the character of God and the range of our own emotions. We had become involved with God and with one another in a new way.

February 27–March 6, 2002

Reflection / Discussion Questions

1. What are contemporary ways people express rage? Which of these are destructive and which are constructive?

2. Ephesians 4:26 is mentioned in the reading and gives Christian instruction regarding anger. How can a person handle his or her anger in such a way as to avoid sin? What is involved in dealing with your anger before the sun goes down?

3. The Bible, as much as it is anything else, is the story of God and the people who have been involved with God. What would help you to be able to read the Bible more faithfully and thus to get involved with God more deeply? What habits can you develop to facilitate this deeper involvement?

4. Reflect on / discuss: Is there anyone with whom you are angry right now? Can you turn that person over to God in prayer so that God may deal with—and perhaps even forgive!—the wrong that he or she may have done to you?

5. Reflect on / discuss: Are there people who may have legitimate laments to God because of you? Are there any wrongs for which you need to repent and make amends, any relationships that need mending?

31

TRUE CONFESSIONS

IN THE FACE of so great and utter a tragedy, too many of the church's pastors committed an offense, by their silence, against the church itself and its mission," declared France's Roman Catholic bishops. "Today we confess that such a silence was a sin. In so doing, we recognize that the church of France failed in her mission as teacher of consciences and that therefore she carries along with the Christian people the responsibility for failing to lend their aid, from the very first moments, when protest and protection were still possible as well as necessary, even if, subsequently, a great many acts of courage were performed."

The bishops read this passage on September 30 as part of a five-page Declaration of Repentance. The bishops' statement was part of a ceremony marking the 57th anniversary of the enactment of anti-Semitic laws under the wartime Vichy government, which collaborated with Nazi occupation troops in France. The ceremony took place near a former Jewish deportation camp in the Paris suburb of Drancy.

The bishops' confession is an extraordinary gesture of public repentance and accountability. Yet it has not been without controversy. Some Jews have complained that it is too little, too late. In their view, such a confession should have been made long before 57 years had passed and made by those directly involved. On the other hand, some French Catholics have criticized the bishops for dwelling on the past and for being too critical of their own people. In their view, such a confession should not have been made at all; we ought to let bygones be bygones. What good is wallowing in guilt?

One can more easily sympathize with the Jewish critique. After all, the acknowledgment *has* taken too long. Moreover, in a time when Western culture seems saturated with self-indulgent people publicly "confessing" their shame while simultaneously excusing it, we have developed a healthy wariness of the motives behind public confession.

Just weeks after the French bishops' declaration, we endured the spectacle of sportscaster Marv Albert's "confession" after he was forced to plead guilty to charges of sexual misconduct. Albert acknowledged regret about what had happened but refused to accept responsibility. "I'm sorry if [the woman] felt she was harmed."

Albert's actions followed a distressingly familiar pattern. When celebrities are discovered to have done something wrong, they find a way to "confess" shame without acknowledging wrongdoing, and then they express the desire to move on with life. The tacit agreement is that the media will then turn their attention to other matters, and the person can disappear for a short while before re-emerging "rehabilitated." Marv Albert will undoubtedly be back on the air within a year, his misdeeds forgotten and, supposedly, "forgiven."

Such transparently false and self-indulgent mea culpas make many of us wary of public confession, and such wariness is healthy. But it would be a mistake to become cynical about every possibility for confession, forgiveness and reconciliation. That is why the French bishops' declaration offers such a powerful witness, even 57 years after the fact.

The bishops do not want to just "let bygones be bygones." They know that reconciliation requires that perpetrators not forget or repress what happened but learn to

142

remember truthfully and graciously. As the declaration states, "The Catholic Church, far from wanting [the planned extermination of the Jewish people by the Nazis] to be forgotten, knows full well that conscience is formed in remembering, and that, just as no individual person can live in peace with himself, neither can society live in peace with a repressed or untruthful memory." The declaration offers a remarkably subtle and truthful account of the complex issues that led so many Christians to be either silent or actively complicit during the Nazi terror.

The bishops state that "we are not ourselves guilty of what took place in the past; but we must be fully aware of the cost of such behavior and such actions." They further acknowledge that Christians bear a "heavy inheritance" toward the Jews, "with all its consequences which are so difficult to wipe out. Hence our still open wounds."

This is not a mea culpa designed for quick rehabilitation and moral amnesia. The bishops recognize that they must accept accountability for the past. They rightly emphasize that conscience must be nurtured through truthful remembering—a remembering that requires costly forgiveness and repentance.

The bishops' confession is shaped by the central Christian conviction that there is no way to Easter except through the events of Maundy Thursday and Good Friday. Easter is not about Christ uncrucified, or sin bypassed and overlooked. It is about Christ crucified and risen, sin confronted and forgiven. Peter is not allowed to forget that he betrays Christ; he is called to remember it in the context of God's Easter people. It is our conscience, formed in remembering the ways people not only are betrayed and are wounded but betray and wound others, that enables us to live into a future not bound by the destructiveness of the past.

Accordingly, the bishops' declaration is a significant gesture, even if it is 57 years late. It is a statement that can help Christians and Jews begin to find ways to heal the open wounds of the past for the sake of the future. Such a confession offers a stark alternative to the shallow confessions and moral amnesia that afflict our culture and our own lives. As the bishops conclude, "This act of remembering calls us to an ever keener vigilance on behalf of humankind today and in the future." Truthful confession and remembrance is difficult—and hopeful—work.

November 19–26, 1997

Reflection / Discussion Questions

1. How does it make you feel to apologize for something? Describe the relationship between apologizing and repenting.
2. The ninth and tenth chapters of the Book of Nehemiah record the public confession and repentance of the people of Israel after their return from Babylonian exile. Read through these chapters, and note how they include the sins of their ancestors from long ago in the confession that precedes their promises to return to obedience. Are there things for which Christians in America corporately need to apologize, past sins that call for public repentance? Explain.
3. Read 2 Corinthians 7:9-11 to find Paul's instructions to the Corinthians on the difference between feelings of worldly grief and godly repentance. How would you describe these two different kinds of reactions? What fruit do they produce?
4. Are there any current social practices that the church encourages or at least tolerates, for which we ought to apologize sooner rather than later? Explain. Do we need to do some repenting of our own racism, or of our atti-

tudes toward abortion, economic social justice, or euthanasia? And if so, in what ways? What lessons can we learn from the WWII-era dehumanizing of whole groups of people?

5. Why is it important to remember and repent rather than just to let bygones be bygones?

32

TRUTH OR CONSEQUENCES

WHEN DAVID HOROWITZ offered 50 college newspapers a paid advertisement, he was setting a perfect trap. College editors across the country had to decide whether or not to publish the ad, which opposes any form of reparations to African-Americans for slavery and racism. If editors turned down his offer, Horowitz could claim that political correctness still reigns on campuses and that major universities are afraid of opposing views on issues of race. If they accepted, Horowitz would get widespread publicity for views that would not otherwise pass editorial muster for accuracy or depth of analysis.

Horowitz got mixed results. Many school newspapers rejected the ad, while a number of others ran it. Some whose editors published it later regretted their decision and issued apologies to their campus communities. Duke's student newspaper, the *Chronicle,* accepted the ad and then defended its decision strongly, mostly on "free speech" grounds.

As a result, the Duke campus became embroiled in a provocative series of protests, debates and discussions, some about journalistic ethics and the problem of using "free speech" to defend the acceptance of a paid advertisement. Other students have addressed the legacies of racism at Duke and challenged administrators to take concrete steps to improve the racial climate and, in the divinity school, to heighten our already strong commitment to racial reconciliation.

We have also examined the underlying issue of reparations and asked ourselves how we might more faithfully work to repair the damage wrought by the legacies of slavery and the reality of racism.

Unfortunately, here in the U.S. we've become preoccupied with the actual logistics of the compensation—how much it would cost, who would pay and who would be eligible to receive payments.

How would the discussions be different if we asked how the United States, as a people, ought to undertake repentance for the past? Horowitz's ad presumes that the issue of reparations is about what "we" (i.e., white Americans) owe to "them" (i.e., black Americans). He uses that bifurcation to defeat the issue by saying things aren't nearly so neatly divided. But what if the question really is about how all of us as a people are to come to terms with the past?

There are dangers in such a question, for many people comfortable with the notion of repentance will use it as an opportunity for infinite guilt with little promise of forgiveness. We must also ask whether, in our individualistic presumptions, we have a sufficient sense of what it means to be a "people."

We should at least be able to ask how Christians in the U.S. ought to undertake repentance. At least in principle, Christians are a people who recognize the call to practice and understand costly forgiveness that induces serious repentance. We have resources that we draw on to capture a deeper understanding of the stakes involved in repairing the past. Yet we are ourselves so broken, and have done so much to trivialize both forgiveness and repentance, that we often mirror the world's confusions.

How can we make a serious theological contribution to the reparations debate in the United States? We can broaden the debate by linking reparations to questions of repentance, forgiveness and a costly reconciliation. But the costs are not only in terms of financial payments. There are several other dimensions we need to identify—ironically, they are dimensions that I have discerned more from observing South Africa's Truth and Reconciliation Commission than through my participation in churches in the U.S.

First, we need a truthful accounting of the past and of the realities of the present. Among the disturbing features of Horowitz's ad are its bizarre and willful distortions of the past. I am not suggesting that we will all reach agreement, but our disagreements need to be shaped by a quest for truthfulness. This excludes both willful distortions and a self-justifying venting that assumes something is true simply because "I feel it" or "I think it."

Second, there needs to be some public remembering of the legacies of slavery and the realities of racism. I realized this when a friend from South Africa asked me why the U.S. has not built memorials to remember the legacies of slavery as it has for such events as the Vietnam war and the Holocaust.

Third, we need to undertake concrete deeds of repentance directed at eradicating racism and healing the brokenness of our past. Though mainline churches led the way in the civil rights movement, today this commitment to racial reconciliation is found more in evangelical traditions than anywhere else.

Fourth, some form of financial reparations is crucial. In the context of these other three dimensions, reparations can avoid being seen either as a "payoff" or an unjustified "theft" of money by others. I am not suggesting a complicated form of payment to specific individuals or families. Reparations might be made through concentrated efforts to invest financially in institutions such as historically black state colleges and universities. We cannot avoid the importance of economic issues if we are to find a future not bound by the past.

If we Christians begin to reclaim the significance of repentance and forgiveness in relation to reparations, Horowitz's ad may, perversely and inadvertently, have offered us a Lenten gift.

May 16, 2001

Reflection / Discussion Questions

1. What other articles or debates about reparations for slavery and racism have you read or heard? What seem to be the main issues and the main arguments both pro and con?

2. Why do you think the United States has not built memorials to remember the legacies of slavery as it has for such events as the Vietnam War and the Holocaust?

3. The reading suggests that the language of repentance, forgiveness, and reconciliation can help us to think theologically about the debate. What does this mean specifically? Who specifically needs to repent, and of what? Who needs to forgive whom for what? What is broken that needs to be reconciled?

4. What biblical examples can you think of that illustrate a similar reconciliation between people? What biblical guidance is available to us in negotiating this complicated theological and political issue? You might consider Zacchaeus's example in Luke 19:1-10. Read through this passage, and discuss how it might be similar to or different from the current reparations debate.

33

CHRISTMAS PRESENCE

THERE WILL BE no Christmas celebration in Bethlehem's Manger Square this year. The annual festivities have been canceled because the organizers have deemed it inappropriate to celebrate in the midst of the conflicts and violence.

It is difficult to understand the political complexities of the Middle East and easy to feel despair about any possible solutions. The loss of a Christmas celebration in Manger Square is a particularly troubling symbol for the region, and a painful sign of the Palestinian plight.

Might it also be a troubling sign theologically, especially for Christians who live outside the Middle East? It is troubling in the first place because so few of us are aware of the plight of our Palestinian Christian brothers and sisters. For too many people, a Palestinian is a terrorist. Palestinian priest Elias Chacour often begins addresses in the United States by opening up his jacket and saying, "I am a Palestinian. I am not a terrorist." Too many of us have an image of Israel and Palestinians that precludes recognition of our historical and contemporary ties to Palestinian followers of Jesus. As a result, we do not recognize what is at stake for a Christian presence in Bethlehem.

Many of us have sentimentalized Christmas in Bethlehem. Dorothy Jean Weaver, an American New Testament scholar currently on sabbatical in Bethlehem, diagnoses the problem in an e-mail newsletter:

It was not an especially pretty world. . . . The Palestine of Jesus' day was a world of grinding poverty for the masses, hard labor for a daily pittance, wealthy tax collectors who made their fortunes by extorting money from the impoverished, and brutal military occupiers whose preferred method of crowd control was crucifixion. . . . Nor was the town of Jesus' birth an especially peaceful place, and hardly the idyllic Bethlehem of our beloved Christmas carol, lying "still" under the "silent stars" in "deep and dreamless sleep."

Weaver then describes present realities: "Two thousand years later the picture looks strangely similar. The Palestine of Christmas 2000 is a world of massive unemployment and growing poverty. And the Bethlehem of Christmas 2000, with its sister cities Beit Jala and Beit Sahour, knows only too well the terrifying sounds and scenes of war."

When we sentimentalize that "little town" of Bethlehem, we also sentimentalize the Jesus who was born there. As Weaver puts it:

When God comes to be with God's people, it is not to an idyllic, fairy-tale world. . . . There would in fact be no need for "God with us" in that "never never" world. The world that Jesus Emmanuel comes to is rather the real world . . . of poverty, extortion, callous cruelty, unrelenting terror and inconsolable grief. It is this world and none other into which God comes to be with us in the person of Jesus, the defenseless child and the crucified Messiah.

Weaver offers a powerful reminder that Christians cannot understand Christmas apart from Good Friday and Easter. An unsentimental Bethlehem, then and now, ought to call us to approach Christmas not only with joyful song but also in a spirit of repentance, forgiveness and faithful witness to God's costly, life-giving love.

Jesus' injunction to love one's enemies is as integral to the celebration of Christmas as it is to Good Friday and Easter. It was no easier then than it is now. Both Jesus' birth—in a dirty manger in the midst of an occupied Bethlehem—and his life of unstinting love challenged established patterns of hatred and bitterness that eventually nailed him to a cross. Yet we are empowered by the giving and forgiving love of Christmas, Good Friday and Easter to love our enemies—especially the concrete enemy who is all too present to us.

Perhaps such understanding might help us stand in solidarity with our Palestinian brothers and sisters while also offering a glimpse of hope for peace among warring peoples in the Middle East. Earlier this fall, Rabbi Michael Lerner offered a courageous vision grounded in his own tradition's high holy day of Yom Kippur:

> Given my own outrage over the killing of Israeli soldiers, this is a moment when it seems easier to just forget my faith and stay in my anger. But I also know that when the Jewish people can only see our own pain, however real and legitimate, it is time to atone.

In the United States we have become so focused on Christmas presents that we have lost sight of the significance of Christmas presence—the presence of the real Jesus, born in the midst of suffering and death in order to announce and embody a kingdom of life even to the point of his own suffering and death. Might it be time for us to repent of our sentimentalized and commercialized Christmas, to atone for the fact that we find it all too easy to celebrate the birth of Christ without seeing anyone's pain? Perhaps we should begin by bearing witness to the tragedy of Christmas being canceled in Bethlehem's Manger Square.

December 20–27, 2000

Reflection / Discussion Questions

1. What traditions do you associate with the celebration of Christmas?

2. On the first Christmas, the Son of God was born directly among the poor and the lowly in a Bethlehem stable. How can your family and congregation, as the gathered body of Christ, celebrate Christmas in a way that is consistent with God's work at the first Christmas?

3. How important is it to you that there continue to be Christians living in the Holy Land, especially in places like Bethlehem? How can we show support for the Palestinian Christians who live there?

4. Although Christians are a people whose holy land can be defined by the location of word, font, and table and not just by geopolitical history, it is nevertheless a tragedy that the land trod by the feet of the Prince of Peace is so badly mired in war and violence that his birth cannot publicly be celebrated there. Reflect on / discuss how we might begin to make steps toward peace and justice in the Middle East.

5. In Matthew 5:43-48, we find Jesus' famous and difficult words about love for our enemies. Read these verses slowly and carefully, and reflect on / discuss how you might be able to act in love toward whoever qualifies as your enemy.

34

A LITTLE FORGETFULNESS

MANY OF US struggle with the burdens of memory. We often wrestle with the presence of horrifying memories whose power paralyzes us from envisioning a better future. We feel trapped by the past. In these cases, a little forgetfulness might help heal psyches and relationships—and even whole societies. This is suggested with particular poignancy in Amos Elon's 1993 essay "The Politics of Memory":

> I have lived in Israel most of my life and have come to the conclusion that where there is so much traumatic memory, so much pain, so much memory innocently or deliberately mobilized for political purposes, a little forgetfulness might finally be in order. This should not be seen as a banal plea to "forgive and forget." Forgiveness has nothing to do with it. While remembrance is often a form of vengeance, it is also, paradoxically, the basis of reconciliation. What is needed, in my view, is a shift in emphasis and proportion, and a new equilibrium in Israeli political life between memory and hope.

What would it mean for people to discover that "a little forgetfulness might finally be in order"? Is it true that forgiveness has "nothing to do with it"?

The dynamics of "so much traumatic memory" converge in our most difficult psychological, social and political dilemmas: in the Middle East, in Bosnia, in South Africa, in racial divisions in the U.S., and in broken and oppressive family relations.

We may have to come to terms with a single episode whose traumatic effects are imprinted in our memories: the murder or suicide of a child, a rape or other sexual assault, a devastating betrayal, a single bomb which destroyed one's home and surroundings.

Or we may struggle with the results of repeated abuse, violence or torture, the effects of which perdure in the soul long after the beatings or the emotional assaults or the violence stop. This is particularly painful when there are permanent marks or wounds left on the body, but no less painful—and perhaps more difficult to identify and treat—when the wounds are imprinted only on the soul.

Third, we may face horrors which have not only assaulted individual people in isolated acts, but which, in their cumulative effect, have so pervaded a culture, a people, that they are passed on from generation to generation. Perhaps nothing has directly happened to a particular person, but his memories are traumatic precisely because of the ways in which the legacies of prior atrocities haunt the present.

Finally, there are events that sear people's memories not because they have happened to us, or to others we love, or to "innocent" strangers, but because *I* or *we* have perpetrated them. An apt example of this is Albert Speer, the Nazi architect and minister of armaments who genuinely sought to repent for his complicity in the Nazi regime. He was unable ever to acknowledge the full force of what he did or admit that he had been aware of the Final Solution—perhaps because he feared that he would have been unable to do so and continue to live.

Living with any of these kinds of memories can cause us to fear our recollections of the past, to devote time and energy to keeping the past at bay.

Yet Christians are called to be a people of memory. Might

it be that, in the working of God's Holy Spirit, the One who is conforming us to the crucified and risen Christ, we can find resources for healing traumatic memories? Despite Elon's comment, forgiveness may have something to do with it.

We proclaim that the risen Christ returns to those who crucified him with a judgment that does not condemn but instead offers new life. But that new life comes through forgiveness and the return of memory, not its erasure or its denial. Christ redeems the past; he does not undo it. The risen Christ bears the wounds of his crucifixion. As Easter people, we believe the past—whatever it is—can be borne. That is why remembering is so central to celebrations of baptism and of the Eucharist and to practices of prayer.

In this life, we must be guided by the memory of sin as a shield against sin, by the memory of Christ's wounds that are in solidarity with all victims who have suffered and those who continue to suffer. We must remember their and our suffering, and we must allow that memory to be spoken out loud for all to hear. But we need to do so in the context of God's forgiveness which, slowly and painfully, heals the past. This can be fostered through liturgies of healing, of baptism, of baptismal renewal, of reconciliation.

What we learn to forget is the past as the occasion for continually festering wounds. As our wounds heal, then perhaps the memories will become less and less painful until they no longer are the source of desires for vengeance. Perhaps the Christian vision of a new Jerusalem, a new heaven and a new earth, can equip us to envision a time when our wounds—and all of the world's wounds—will have been fully healed. Miroslav Volf suggests that such a vision offers us "a divine gift of nonremembrance."

Scriptural references emphasize that God will "blot out your transgressions" and "will not remember your sin" (Isa. 43:25; Jer. 31:34), and the Book of Revelation refers to the "first things passing away" with the arrival of a new heaven and the new earth. These texts refer to a transformation in which we will learn to remember our histories, even in their ugliness, in a way that *we need not* remember them as sin because they have been fully healed.

As we struggle with searing memories, a little nonremembrance is in order. But only because that nonremembrance has everything to do with the gracious work of God's forgiveness.

February 4–11, 1998

Reflection / Discussion Questions

1. Are you more likely to remember an incident wherein you have been treated fairly or unfairly? Explain your answer.
2. Describe the difference between forgetting and forgiving. In Matthew 18:21-22, Peter asks Jesus if he ought to forgive a sinful brother as many as seven times. When Jesus figuratively increases this amount beyond counting, what is he teaching about memory and forgiveness?
3. Are there people who have wronged you whom you need to forgive? Are there people of whom you are aware who are still seared with a memory of a wrong you have committed? What can you do to reconcile these kinds of relationships?

35

A BOTTOMLESS PIT

"THE POLITICS OF death is a bottomless pit that sucks everybody in." This judgment, offered by a California attorney who has tried more than 100 capital cases, aptly summarizes the complicated arguments for and against the death penalty in American culture. After all, who can deny the horrors of a Ted Bundy or a Jeffrey Dahmer? Who can deny the pain of parents whose children are slaughtered by unrepentant murderers? Yet how many innocent people have died in the midst of a politics of revenge? How do we account for racial and economic disparities among those sentenced to death? And what do we tell ourselves and our children, if the way we respond to murder is by killing the murderer?

The attorney's judgment also summarizes my reaction after reading a gripping true narrative, *Dead Run: The Untold Story of Dennis Stockton and America's Only Mass Escape from Death Row*. Authors Joe Jackson and William F. Burke Jr. tell the story of Dennis Stockton, a man who they believe was wrongly convicted and executed. They narrate in excruciating detail the sordid character of life on death row and the inmates' encounters with prison guards, wardens, attorneys and others.

Part of what makes their account so gripping is that they rely on diaries that Stockton kept throughout his time in Virginia's Mecklenburg Correctional Facility. The diaries provide an "insider's account" of living and dying on death row. They also reveal the planning that led to a mass escape from death row in 1983 (Stockton declined to participate in this escape), as well as Stockton's reflections as his appeals ran out and he faced his final days in 1995.

Jackson and Burke undertake some investigative reporting to analyze Stockton's claim to innocence, a claim that they come to believe and that I found persuasive. They do not excuse Stockton's other criminal behavior, and they include a candid analysis of the mess Stockton made of his life. But they are convinced that he was innocent of the crime for which he was put on death row.

Jackson and Burke also reflect on the politics of the death penalty in Virginia and offer a provocative account of its relation to slavery. They point out that Virginia has had many more executions than, for example, North Carolina. They argue that a significant reason for this is that Virginia was more dependent on slaves and that the punitive system of slavery was easily transmuted into legalized desires for vengeance through the death penalty.

As I read their account, I developed an intense despair about the politics of death. There are few heroes in this story. Stockton and his associates engage in regular criminal behavior and are often drunk or high on drugs. The prosecutors who try the case appear to be more interested in higher office than in justice. The prison guards, underpaid and overworked, are susceptible to bribes and other corruption. The legal system is constrained by stringent laws that do not provide adequate safeguards to protect innocent people from being executed. Several of the other men on death row, as described by their fellow inmate, are truly frightening characters. In this story, the politics of death is a bottomless pit that sucks everybody in.

Is there any hope? Glimmers can be found in some of Stockton's regret about decisions he made, in the attorneys who represent Stockton in his final appeals because they believe in his innocence, and in the reporters themselves. But even the attorneys and the reporters become discouraged and despondent when Stockton is executed. Jackson and Burke comment poignantly in their epilogue: "Who could tell the truth from the lies? In the end, the only certainty was that the true story surrounding the murder of Kenny Arnder that warm July night in 1978 might never be revealed. The law's purpose had shifted from the search for truth to the triumph of procedure. The lawyers argued law, and society looked away."

Might there be more hope if society would stop looking away? Or to put it less abstractly, if you and I stopped looking away? Do we look away because we fear the bottomless pit? Or because we do not want to confront our own complicity in systems of punishment that dehumanize us all—prisoners, lawyers and prison officials included? Have we confronted not just the abstract arguments about capital punishment, but the actual conditions of our prisons and the persons within them—including the chilling character of many of the prisoners?

Christians are enjoined by Jesus to visit those in prison, but how many of us do so? A few years ago, I was taken aback when a woman came to visit me to ask why Christians were so unforgiving. She had heard that I had written a book on forgiveness, and she was trying to figure out why so many churches were unwilling to interact with recently paroled ex-convicts. She worked in the attorney general's office, assigned to help reintegrate ex-convicts into the community. Yet she had found churches in her area to be consistently resistant to reaching out. She told me that she was a Christian, but that she found it increasingly difficult to believe that the gospel actually made much difference in the world or in people's lives.

Her question about why Christians are so unforgiving has haunted me. Could it be that the only way to avoid the bottomless pit of our politics of death is to think through and embody the complex practices involved in the redemptive forgiveness of Christ? There, we claim, a politics of life is to be found—of life abundant and free. Are we willing to risk a justice that is restorative rather than merely retributive?

March 8, 2000

Reflection / Discussion Questions

1. What do you know about capital punishment law and practice in your state? What do you know about attempts at reform that are underway in many states?
2. The end of the reading mentions the possibility of restorative justice instead of merely retributive justice. Take a moment to describe your understanding of these two different approaches to justice. What are the advantages and risks of each? Do you think God's justice as shown to us by Jesus can be classified as one or the other? Explain.
3. Ancient Israelite law recorded in the Old Testament provides for capital punishment for a number of crimes. The New Testament never addresses the issue in any direct way, other than in Jesus' example and the words of the Sermon on the Mount. How should the Bible shape our ethical discernment about capital punishment?
4. Read the opening verses of Luke 15 for an example of the scandal caused by Jesus' insistence on consorting with outcasts and sinners in society. The reading alludes to the need to turn our attention to the real people and situations of our prisons and correctional systems. How might we compare current convicted criminals with the people around Jesus? How might such a turning of our attention shape our attitudes and public practices around directives to visit those in prison, as well as larger issues about capital punishment?

36

TOUGH LOVE
FOR SEXUAL ABUSERS

Hᴏᴡ ᴅᴏ ᴡᴇ handle clergy sexual misconduct faithfully and compassionately? The issues and challenges extend
far beyond any one crisis and indict all churches that have
failed to recognize the complexity of those issues and faithfully engage them.

My wife served for four challenging years on the committee that dealt with clergy sexual misconduct in her United
Methodist Church conference. The committee tended to
oscillate between two extreme postures: sweeping the
offense under the rug as if nothing had happened, or adopt-
ing a harshly punitive stance that seemed to ignore any
prospect of forgiveness and reconciliation. How, my wife
wondered, can the church offer a distinctive witness to the
importance of taking sin seriously—thereby ensuring
accountability—while also embodying the power of costly
forgiveness?

Unfortunately, we have often failed to handle the situations appropriately, let alone to demonstrate a distinctive
witness. This failure has become even more troubling as we
hear about horrifying sexual misconduct by Roman Catholic
priests and cover-ups by church officials. The number and
gravity of the offenses make it clear that these are systemic
problems that must be addressed.

Some of the problems are peculiar to pedophilia, a problem that is resistant to cure and typically results in repeat offenses. Medical and mental health professionals on the one hand, and church officials on the other, have failed to take appropriate steps to protect people—and especially children and teenagers—from pedophiles and ephebophiles. People are rightly angry and outraged.

When criminal wrongdoing is apparent or even suspected, the appropriate civil authorities need to be notified and engaged. Further, we ought to ensure that victims (or potential victims) of misconduct are protected and supported. This will involve removing offenders from positions of public authority and sacred trust. Our first concern needs to be to care for those who have been sinned against, even as we honor the possibility that persons may be wrongly accused.

At the same time, we need to keep in view a larger horizon. That horizon is not a cheap and distorting sense of forgiveness, in which perpetrators are let off the hook and set free to commit sin again. But neither is it a nihilism, one that presumes that once you fall there is no redemption.

Rather, the horizon is shaped by the costly forgiveness of Christ's cross and resurrection. Several Catholic bishops asked parish priests to address the crisis in their Palm Sunday services. Ironically, the timing of this request seemed to have a lot to do with how events were unfolding in the media. But situating this reflection at the beginning of Holy Week was uncannily appropriate, for the drama of Christ's betrayal, crucifixion and resurrection is key to a coherent and faithful response to clergy sexual misconduct.

There are at least six lessons to be learned from these crises. First, sin must be confronted—not ignored. Sin is too pervasive and subtle for us to be able to evade its reality. We must grapple not only with isolated cases of wrongdoing, but with sin as a reality that grips us in our thoughts and desires as well as our actions.

Second, we learn that the past can be redeemed. We do

not worship Christ uncrucified; we worship Christ crucified and risen. When the risen Christ returns to the disciples, he does not forget the past, but he does redeem it as he calls them to new life.

Third, the means by which the past is redeemed is costly. We cannot afford cheap grace, nor can we trivialize the difficulty in unlearning sin and learning how to live differently. The risen Christ returns with a judgment that offers new life. Yet it is still judgment.

Fourth, while Christ's death and resurrection offer us forgiveness, the only way we can appropriately receive that forgiveness is by undertaking repentance. We learn the true liberation of forgiveness when we commit ourselves not to replicate the past but to live into a different future. This repentance also leads us to turn to our own victims and to live in solidarity with victimized people everywhere.

Fifth, we need to be able to claim that we are all sinners without claiming that all sins are equivalent. Betrayals of trust, especially in the midst of power differentials and by people in whom sacred authority has been vested, are especially grievous sins that call for clear accountability and expectations of true repentance.

Finally, Christ calls us to love our enemies—even without their repentance. This "tough love" will provide clear accountability and a policy of "zero tolerance" for wrongdoing. But it is love nonetheless. Yes, to presume that the fullness of forgiveness and reconciliation is possible without authentic repentance is to cheapen grace. But to withhold love and close off reconciliation is, as Jonah discovered, to isolate ourselves from God.

Can we respond to clergy sexual misconduct in ways that hold together outrage, accountability, forgiveness and the possibility of reconciliation and new life? Can we "love enemies" in ways that avoid the nihilism of unforgivable wrongdoing and unredeemable wrongdoers?

These are daunting challenges, but they urgently need to

be confronted. Even more, they embody a distinctive witness to the power of Christ's cross and resurrection—with all of its costly love and pain and hope and forgiveness.

April 24–May 1, 2002

Reflection / Discussion Questions

1. Most of us are aware of cases of sexual harassment or other forms of sexual misconduct in a variety of contexts. Is sexual misconduct by Christian clergy different? If so, how? How does the betrayal of trust hurt people beyond the actual actions?
2. Discuss the six lessons briefly described in the second half of the reading. How would these principles guide your actions in a concrete situation?
3. Paul wrote to the Corinthians about dealing with some particularly egregious sins in their congregation. Read 1 Corinthians 5:1-5 and 2 Corinthians 2:5-11. What seem to be the concerns and priorities that shape Paul's advice in these two situations?

PART 5

A HOPEFUL FUTURE

37

EVIL AND GOOD FRIDAY

A PASTOR FROM South Africa was finishing his first year as a full-time pastor in the U.S. He had served churches in the two countries, so I asked him to compare the role of the church in the U.S. with its role in South Africa.

"I am still trying to come to terms," he said, "with a culture where Mother's Day and Father's Day are more obligatory days of church attendance than is Good Friday."

"In South Africa," he went on, "we have experienced so much suffering and evil that Good Friday is a pivotal day for us. We cannot understand the hope of Easter apart from confronting the pain and agony of Good Friday. But in America people come to church on Palm Sunday and again on Easter, with no services in between. Yet the church was packed on Mother's Day!"

My friend was troubled not only that so few people attend church on Good Friday, but that U.S. churches and church-related institutions often do not consider Good Friday a holiday. Why is Good Friday so unimportant for mainstream Protestant Christianity in America?

My friend's words haunt me, for they point to an impoverished set of cultural and ecclesial resources for grappling with evil. While in recent years many Americans have not had as much firsthand engagement with massive suffering and evil as have South Africans, we are aware of the images of massive horror within our own country and around the world: school shootings and other mass murders, racial violence, civil wars, and on it goes.

Yet we have difficulty naming and identifying, much less explaining, the significance of these events. We have lost the vocabulary for describing the realities we confront. As American cultural analyst Andrew Delbanco puts it in his provocative book *The Death of Satan*, "The repertoire of evil has never been richer. Yet never have our responses been so weak. We have no language for connecting our inner lives with the horrors that pass before our eyes in the outer world." Why?

Delbanco proposes that we have undergone an extensive process of "unnaming evil," a process that goes back at least a couple of centuries but which has "accelerated enormously" over the past 50 years. He traces the loss of the language of Satan, of evil and even of sin, from the American cultural vocabulary.

To be sure, Delbanco does not offer an oversimplified narrative. He describes diverse intellectual, cultural, social and theological forces that converge to diminish evil as a part of America's imaginative vocabulary.

Delbanco believes that this process of "unnaming evil" has left us deeply troubled. "Despite the monstrous uses to which Satan has been put, I believe that our culture is now in crisis because evil remains an inescapable experience for all of us, while we no longer have a symbolic language for describing it."

Delbanco offers a powerful analysis, yet I am troubled by one part of his conclusion: In what sense is evil an "inescapable experience for all of us"? Isn't part of the problem that many modern Western people, Christians and non-Christians alike, have found it too easy to deny that evil is an experience for "me" or "us"? It is always somewhere else. People are exposed to massive horror through television and other media. But does such exposure do anything more than make us voyeurs of others' suffering?

Could it be that our impoverished cultural and ecclesial resources conspire with modern media to make evil apparent but fundamentally unreal? Are we aware of evil's reality yet blind to its force and effects, unable to name and describe it?

Obviously, South Africa's experience of profound suffering and trauma gives rise to struggles for which the liturgy of Good Friday offers voice. So it is unsurprising that so many South African Christians are drawn to church on Good Friday. It expresses powerfully people's concrete struggles with evil and suffering.

Yet the dynamic also works in the other direction. The Good Friday liturgy can shape and reshape our engagement with the reality of evil and provide a vocabulary for describing it. Good Friday confronts us with evil as an "inescapable experience for all of us." We are compelled to reflect on evil as a reality that cuts through our own lives, our own hearts and minds, imaginations and actions. We ask ourselves, "Is it I, Lord?"

Further, Good Friday provides an opportunity to challenge the superficiality of American optimism that so easily turns into cynicism. It does so by inviting Christians to discover the profound hope of Easter that comes only on the far side of sin and evil, a hope that enables us to see the world and ourselves more truthfully and redemptively.

In Wallace Stegner's novel *Crossing to Safety,* two women visit a museum in Italy and see Piero della Francesca's resurrected Christ rising up from the tomb. The narrator describes the painting: "That gloomy, stricken face permitted no forgetful high spirits. It was not the face of a god reclaiming his suspended immortality, but the face of a man who until a moment ago had been thoroughly and horribly dead, and still had the smell of death in his clothes and the terror of death in his mind."

The two women's reactions were starkly different. One didn't like the painting. The narrator describes her as "still developing her sundial theory of art, which would count no hours but the sunny ones." But the other woman, who had come to terms with the reality of suffering and evil in her own life, pondered the painting for a while. The narrator provides a powerful description of the importance of Good Friday for our vision, our vocabulary and our lives: "She studied it soberly with something like recognition or acknowledgment in her eyes, as if those who have been dead understand things that will never be understood by those who have only lived."

April 12, 2000

Reflection / Discussion Questions

1. What does it say about our culture that Mother's Day is a more obligatory day of worship than Good Friday? Which days of the year seem to be the biggest events in your worship life? In the worship life of your congregation?

2. Read Mark 15 for an account of Jesus' last Friday. Do you regularly attend Good Friday worship services? How do you feel about Good Friday? What connections do you make between the suffering and death of Jesus Christ and the rampant suffering and evil all over our world? What about the suffering and deaths in your own life?

3. Beginning on September 11, 2001, the identification of evil, evil people, and evil regimes became suddenly more common in American conversations both public and private. Do you think this change has been more helpful or more unhelpful? Why? How?

38

LIGHT IN DARKNESS

O N SEPTEMBER 11, I was scheduled to lecture on Simone Weil's classic essay, "The Love of God and Affliction." I never made it to class—it was canceled due to the devastating, horrifying news of the World Trade Center attacks. We immediately organized a prayer service for the divinity school community—but what could be said, even in the context of prayer? What words could explain my own feelings, and especially the pain of those affected directly and the pain experienced by friends and colleagues frantically trying to get in touch with loved ones in New York City? How could I name the emptiness, the pain, the horror?

I returned to Weil's essay, which describes affliction as a condition deeper and more painful than suffering. "Affliction is an uprooting of life, a more or less attenuated equivalent of death, made irresistibly present to the soul by the attack or immediate apprehension of physical pain." According to Weil, a French thinker who was writing in the bleak days of World War II, the physical, psychological and social dimensions of affliction converge to create a horror that seizes the soul.

Those of us in North Carolina were far removed from the physical pain of the attacks—but we identified vicariously through the televised pictures. A key passage in Weil's essay articulates the experience and the challenge we faced: "Affliction makes God appear to be absent for a time, more absent than a dead man, more absent than light in the utter darkness of a cell. A kind of horror submerges the whole soul. During this absence there is nothing to love. What is terrible is that if, in this darkness where there is nothing to love, the soul ceases to love, God's absence becomes final. The soul has to go on loving in the emptiness, or at least to go on wanting to love, though it may only be with an infinitesimal part of itself. Then, one day, God will come to show himself to this soul and to reveal the beauty of the world to it, as in the case of Job. But if the soul stops loving it falls, even in this life, into something almost equivalent to hell."

As events unfolded through the day, it became clear to our divinity school community that we needed to "go on wanting to love." We had not really experienced affliction, but "affliction" described the reality we were trying to understand. But how would the prayer service name our attempt to go on loving, or at least wanting to love?

We focused on three biblical passages. The first, from the opening verses of John's Gospel, included the words we read as we lit a candle of peace, hope and justice on the altar table. The candle—surrounded by barbed wire—had been given to us by South African Christians and had been a key symbol of hope in the midst of the bleakest times of apartheid oppression.

John's Gospel begins with an affirmation of Christ as the one by whom and through whom life and light are found. I spoke the words from my soul as they passed by my lips: "What has come into being in him was life, and the life was the light of all people. The light shines in the darkness, and the darkness did not overcome it" (John 1:3b-5).

Yet even as we lit the candle and spoke the words, we wondered whether the darkness had overcome the light. We turned to the Book of Lamentations: "My soul is bereft of peace; I have forgotten what happiness is; so I say 'Gone is my glory, and all that I had hoped for from the Lord' " (Lam. 3:17-18).

These words named the emptiness we were feeling. Even so, we continued to read: "But this I call to mind, and therefore I have hope. The steadfast love of the LORD never ceases, his mercies never come to an end; they are new every morning; great is your faithfulness. 'The LORD is my portion,' says my soul, 'therefore I will hope in him' " (Lam. 3:21-24).

After an extended period of silence and intercessory prayer, we concluded with words from Psalm 23: "Even though I walk through the darkest valley, I fear no evil; for you are with me; your rod and your staff—they comfort me."

The pain, the emptiness, the horror remained—and will remain for some time to come. But as we continue to gather together, we realize that we go on wanting to love and that we continue to find words to name our hope. We also sang together in the service and discovered the power of music to stir our souls in ways that words alone cannot. As I felt the music enveloping us in praise and love, I wondered: could that praise inspire us, offer us new energy to reach out to others?

I did not anticipate the anxiety I felt as the service ended and the chapel emptied. The candle continued to burn. I did not want to extinguish the flame. The service was over; the symbolism had been powerful. But I wanted to be sure that the light would continue to shine in the darkness, even in its symbolic form.

I finally came to terms with the flame going out, but only in the hope that the hundreds of people who had gathered for prayer in the midst of affliction had departed with a portion of that flame, going forth into the world to bear witness to the light. And only in the hope that countless others will also bear witness to the light and go on wanting to love.

October 17, 2001

Reflection / Discussion Questions

1. Do you remember where you were on the morning of September 11, 2001? Do you remember the first time afterward that you gathered in prayer with other Christians? What was it like?

2. Simone Weil writes of "going on wanting to love" even in the midst of affliction. What does this mean to you? How can love sustain us in, and even draw us through, our times of affliction?

3. John 1:5 says that the light shines in the darkness and that the darkness has not overcome it. Sometimes the word translated as "overcome" is also translated as "understood," and the Gospel writer John may well have intended just such a double meaning. In what ways does a lack of understanding about Jesus characterize the darkness that opposes but does not overcome the Light of the World?

4. What can you and your Christian community do to let the light of Christ shine in you even in times of darkness, so that others may see your love and give glory to God?

39

SHAPED BY LAMENT AND HOPE

L ET'S FACE IT," my clergy friend said to me. "We clergy are much better with people after they are dead than when they are dying. We know how to do funerals. But we find it very difficult to be present with and to care for people at the end of life."

My friend spoke these words as we discussed what a divinity school might do to begin focusing more clearly on caring for people as they face death. Because of broad changes in medical care and in our culture, more and more people are reaching adulthood without ever having been present when someone has died. I asked a group of 60 undergraduates how many of them had watched someone die or been present shortly thereafter. These students would have a sensory appreciation of the reality of death. Only one student raised her hand.

Yet it has not always been that way. In earlier periods and in other cultures, care for the dying has been a ritual focus for families, friends and other loved ones in a community. Stories and paintings dramatically portray the presence of a community caring for the dying. By contrast to earlier periods, where paintings depict a dying person surrounded by close friends, a typical contemporary portrait would have the dying person surrounded by medical equipment.

What has occasioned this difference? In part, it is a result of the widespread denial and evasion of death in our culture.

This has been exacerbated by a youth-oriented culture of progress in which any sign of aging or decay is seen as a threat to be avoided.

Further, contemporary medicine has been focused more on curing than on caring. Indeed, too many doctors see a patient's death as a sign of failure. Recently, as a dying patient was moved from the hospital into a hospice, a resident asked the attending physician: "Why are we giving up?" The resident believed that the physicians should have remained optimistic that they could cure the patient, despite the fact that it was clear the patient was dying.

Our dominant cultural and medical approaches to suffering and death are characterized by complaint and optimism. People tend to be optimistic that any illness or wound can be treated and cured. If for some reason that does not seem possible, we shift into a mode of complaint—complaint about the pain being endured, complaint that medical technology has not progressed rapidly enough, complaint that we are not devoting enough resources to saving the lives of those we care about.

As a result, our medical practice, our cultural expectations and even our training as clergy converge so that we continually intervene to try to cure people all the way to their dying breath. It is no wonder, then, that such a disproportionate percentage of our medical resources is spent on people during the last six months of their lives. Nor is it any wonder that, despite its horrific ethical and theological implications, physician-assisted suicide has begun to attract sympathetic attention. We somehow fear that the only alternatives we have are either costly intervention up to the point of death, or a seemingly compassionate physician-assisted suicide. If those are the only options, then it should not surprise us that Jack Kevorkian could appear to some to be a sympathetic hero.

Fortunately, there are alternatives for those who want to provide better care for the dying. In *Practicing Our Faith,*

Amy Platinga Pauw notes that the Christian practice of dying well should be shaped not by complaint and optimism, but by lament and hope. We can draw on centuries of Christian wisdom and faithful practice to nourish a commitment to dying well and caring for the dying.

In addition to alternative practices of caring for the dying, Christians can also draw on alternative institutional contexts. Hospice care has emerged in recent decades as an important movement offering first-rate medical, nursing and pastoral care for the dying. More and more patients and families are receiving the gift of competent, thoughtful care from both in-patient and home health-care hospices. The poignant stories of families who have received effective and compassionate care for their dying loved ones offer a compelling contrast to the tragedies of lonely patients dying surrounded by machines, and the horrors of people dying at the hands of Kevorkian and other well-intentioned but ultimately misguided physicians.

We face significant medical, ecclesial and cultural obstacles to recovering the practice of dying well. In 1997, only about 400,000 dying people received hospice care out of almost 1.6 million people who would have been appropriate candidates. The median stay for people in hospice was less than three weeks, even though hospices are equipped to provide as much as six months' worth of care. Almost 40 percent of those people who did enter hospice had still not been told they were dying at the time they were admitted. More broadly, churches and families are less directly involved in the care of the dying than they have been in previous generations.

Recovering the practice of dying well will require attention to cultural, economic, theological, ethical and policy issues. It will also involve reshaping our theological, medical and nursing education, drawing on Christian wisdom and insights to provide better care for dying persons and their families.

Christians are called to reclaim and sustain practices of caring as well as curing, of being present with the dying at the bedside even when we know that the news we bring is not what the patient wants to hear. We are called to be people of lament and hope rather than complaint and optimism. And, above all, Christian clergy ought to be as gifted in caring for the dying as in providing funerals for the dead.

April 14, 1999

Reflection / Discussion Questions

1. Have you ever had any experiences with hospice care? If so, what did you learn about the process of dying? What should a congregation's role be at this time in a person's life?
2. Many hospitals were originally founded by religious organizations. Do you agree with the claim that "contemporary medicine has been focused more on curing than caring"? How can the church help reclaim the connection between curing and caring?
3. What are the differences between complaint and lament? Between optimism and hope?
4. In the Bible, death is not represented as being a part of God's original intent for the creation. In 1 Corinthians 15:55, Paul quotes the prophet Hosea and declares victory over death in Christ. How do Christians understand death in the light of sin and redemption? What can we say about God's relationship to human death?

40

GEOGRAPHIES OF MEMORY

IT JUST DIDN'T seem right, reflecting on my father's life and death in the midst of a city where neither of us had spent much time. There were no familiar places that stirred memories of time together, no specific places where I could go to recall the significant events surrounding his death. I was thousands of miles away from his grave. Yet it was July 18, the date on which my father had died and a day that I now mark as a time of mourning and thanksgiving for my parents.

Why did it seem so strange to mark this time without a sense of place? After all, we think of memory as something that resides in our heads, and so we carry our memories around with us—even when we travel to unfamiliar places. But it did seem strange, precisely because memory is not *only* "in our heads." Specific places are significant carriers of our pasts; they are geographies of memory. Specific places evoke powerful emotions and thoughts that flood our hearts and minds with resonances we cannot anticipate. They recall times of inexplicable joy as well as unbearable pain and sadness.

Our memories are often tied to particular places. We were living in that house, in this city, when our first child was born. We were on that bridge, in this resort city, when we decided to get married. It was at that spot, on this mountain, that he slipped and tumbled to his death. It was in that church, the one on the corner, that my parents were married . . .

Unsurprisingly, we want to return to the sites of joyous memories and avoid those that cause significant pain. Yet, although there are sites for each of these memories, there are also sites that evoke a complex mixture of memories that are difficult to disentangle. A friend of mine loves to return to the town where he was raised and nurtured because his parents are buried there, but he is acutely aware that the same town is also the site of physical and psychological racist blows that he has struggled with throughout life. A house can be the site of one child's birth and another's suicide, of beautiful family gatherings as well as horrifying emotional or physical violence. How do we deal with the complex memories that flood through our lives when we return to these sites?

In addition to marking the places that shape our memories, we construct new spaces to locate memories. That is at least part of what we do with cemeteries and gravestones: we create spaces to mark the memories of loved ones who have died. The Tomb of the Unknown Soldier has become a collective space where we give thanks for the sacrifices of those we could not otherwise identify by name.

When we erect monuments and memorials as a public tribute to specific events, they begin to reshape our memories. A firefighter's memorial recalls the sacrifices particular people made so that others can live. A statue evokes the reconciling friendship between two groups of people who had previously been enemies.

The Vietnam Veterans Memorial holds and carries extraordinary memories. A veteran friend of mine spends as much time as he can at the wall. He locates names and recalls friendships, cries over the physical and emotional wounds he continues to bear, grieves about the rejection he felt when he returned, repents of the killings he committed in the war. Visiting the memorial, he says, offers a catharsis that makes it easier to live through the rest of the year.

Some sites are the location of significant healing—or the source of a renewed passion for vengeance. The site where a key leader was killed is preserved in order to mobilize people to "never forget" what has been done to them. A battlefield of defeat becomes the rallying cry for vengeance.

We Christians have our own geographies of memory, especially as we are raised in particular places as members of specific families and ethnic and cultural communities. Yet deep in our tradition there is also a sense of people being in mission, of not being tied to particular places. Is that an invitation to the rootlessness that can all too easily flip over into a pernicious tribalism?

Or might it be that, for Christians, our most determinative geographies of memory are not particular places so much as the specific spaces of pulpit, baptismal font, eucharistic table? Could it be that in worship we locate our memories in the story of God and begin to discover thanksgiving and healing there? We are called to be less attached to the building than to the activities by which our memories are shaped, reshaped and—over time—healed, redeemed and made new. In our study and proclamation of scripture, we ought to be disciplining our memory through learning the story of God. The baptismal font ought to remind us of who and whose we are in ways that enable us to give thanks for particular histories even as we overcome their destructive features. The eucharistic table signifies the ways in which God "remembers" us as we remember the night on which he was betrayed.

At the heart of our faith is an invitation to remember the past differently thanks to the gracious love of God manifested in the crucified and risen Christ. We are invited to place our memories' wounds in the wounds of Christ and to give thanks for our joyous memories by commemorating all the saints, especially those who from their labors rest. To be sure, the movable sites of Christian worship do not erase other sites as carriers of powerful memories. But they relativize the significance of particular places, and offer a more determinative geography for our memories.

July 18th didn't seem right, at least for much of the day, because I was in an unfamiliar place. But when I went to a chapel service, and heard the scripture read and proclaimed, and saw the font and the table, I began to remember again, and to give thanks.

August 30–September 6, 2000

Reflection / Discussion Questions

1. Reflect on / share a memory you hold of a special or significant place from your childhood. Have you ever visited sites from your childhood after years of geographical separation? What memories were triggered by the experience?

2. What specific prayers or scripture readings do you remember that were a part of special worship services in your life, such as weddings, funerals, or baptisms? Do you have recollections of word, font, or table that continue to shape the way you remember those events?

3. Genesis 22:1-14 contains the amazing story of the near sacrifice of Isaac. In verse 14, Abraham gives a special name to the place where these events took place, and it shaped the way that both he and others remembered God from that day forward. Read this story from Genesis and reflect on / discuss the specific locations in your past that bear specific memories of your experience with God.

41

BESIDE THE WEARY ROAD

Even for those faithful souls for whom Christmas begins on December 25 and continues for 12 days thereafter, the season is over. Epiphany has come and gone, the trees have been carted out to the street, and the boxes and gifts have been put away. The dog days of January and February have set in.

Every year in early January, someone tells me that he wishes we could keep the Christmas spirit alive throughout the year. I heard it again a few days ago. I understand the sentiment, but I fear that it reflects more sentimentality than an authentically Christmas spirit.

After all, for many people the "season" of Christmas—that time from late November until Christmas Day—is actually a time of acute pain, loneliness and even despair. This is true of people who don't fit into our culture's celebrations of family, community, and giving and receiving expensive gifts. It is especially true for those who have experienced a death or tragedy during December in any year, as well as those who have recently lost a loved one. For these people, the culture's unabashed celebrations only intensify the pain and grief that they have otherwise been able to manage.

A few days before Christmas my wife and I went to visit a dear friend whose husband died earlier this year. We went in part because of our own sadness that this was the first year in which our friend would not be alive on Christmas Day. We wanted to share some special time with his wife.

We arrived to find her in remarkably good spirits. Only later did we learn part of the reason why. A few nights earlier, she had gone to a midweek service in a neighboring city. It was called "A Worship Service for Those with Hurting Hearts." She described how healing the service had been and said that she now felt ready for Christmas.

On the cover of the worship bulletin was the third verse of "It Came Upon a Midnight Clear." I had never pondered the significance of the beautiful words by Edward Sears: "And ye, beneath life's crushing load, whose forms are bending low, / who toil along the climbing way with painful steps and slow, / Look now! for glad and golden hours come swiftly on the wing. / O rest beside the weary road, and hear the angels sing!"

Through a service designed for "hurting hearts," sufferers could hear the angels sing in a new way, precisely because they had been invited to rest beside the weary road and acknowledge the crushing load of grief. They had not been left alone nor compelled to pretend that they felt the same happiness and joy that others felt at Christmas parties and concerts. Their pain was acknowledged, providing a context for more authentic joy and peace.

Our friend told us that many people gathered for that service. I could only imagine the stories that brought people there—the death of a loved one, the loss of a job, a family breakup, a significant betrayal or deception, the pain inflicted by a violent crime, an accumulation of little stresses that finally had crushed the spirit. Or perhaps it was the sadness of not being able to conceive when so many people around them were celebrating family and the birth of a child. Or maybe it was trying to deal with having been an "unwanted child" in the midst of celebrating perhaps the most wanted child in human history. Whatever their stories, they gathered to listen for the angels to sing beside their weary roads.

A few days after Christmas we visited with another friend who had gone through a painful separation during the previous year. It had been a very difficult time, and she was struggling with feelings of guilt as well as sadness. She was trying to find a sense of hope for the future, but the "Christmas season" had been hard.

We knew this friend loved music, so we had given her a copy of the Duke Chapel Choir singing Handel's *Messiah*. We did not realize how important the words would be to her celebration of Christmas. When we saw her after Christmas, she told us that the phrase, "He has borne our sorrows," had offered her great consolation and comfort. Such phrases and the music had helped her to recognize again that the one whose birth we celebrate is none other than the one who bears our sorrows and heals our pain.

This is the spirit of Christmas that we must retain throughout the year and throughout our lives. What would this look like for us? What would happen if we believed that Christmas is less a day or season of the year and more a way of living faithful to the God whose giving and forgiving love is manifest in Jesus Christ?

In part, it means following the tradition of Handel's *Messiah,* the carols, the pietàs that show Mary's tears, the Gospels that draw together the story of the baby in the manger with the ministry, death and resurrection of Jesus of Nazareth. But it might also mean singing a hymn like "Love Came Down at Christmas" in the middle of July.

Perhaps, most deeply, it calls us to develop the capacity to hear the angels sing throughout the year, whether beside life's weary road or from the mountaintops of life's great accomplishments. In music and liturgies that touched their hearts, our friends found a deeper understanding of Christmas and of the God whom we worship. When we learn to listen for the angels amidst the full range of life's joys and griefs, hopes and fears, then perhaps we will also rediscover a profoundly Christmas spirit.

January 31, 2001

Reflection / Discussion Questions

1. Are there any painful holiday memories that linger from year to year for you or someone you love? What do you think the church could do to embody the love of Christ in such a situation?
2. What hymns or other pieces of Christian music hold special value for you in ways similar to the situations of the two women described in this reading? Explain the significance.
3. What friends or colleagues do you know who are struggling with loss or pain and who could really use a companion to sit with them on the mourning bench beside the weary road? How can you reach out in Christian love at this time?
4. What ways can you think of for your congregation to plan worship that would acknowledge the wounds of the hurting and to support the wounded in the love of God?
5. At Christmas we remember that Mary herself had a song to sing about God's mercy to the humble and the hungry. Read and reflect on / discuss Mary's "Magnificat" in Luke 1:46-55. How can this scripture guide you and your congregation as you "rediscover a profoundly Christmas spirit"?

42

WHY ARE THEY SINGING?

OUR HOSTS in Estonia were somberly describing the challenges they faced in maintaining a Christian presence throughout the Soviet era. One Methodist district superintendent had been deported to Siberia during the Stalin era and then executed. The KGB was regularly present at their church gatherings, watching suspiciously to see what was going on.

Then one older leader of the church, a minister, smiled. "Let me tell you how little they understood us, and how little they could understand people's deep longings for God's love." He described how the church people would often disguise their time for Christian education with the children, fearing that the KGB would use their catechesis as an excuse to arrest church members. "Yet," he added, "they just didn't get it. We couldn't disguise the children's love for singing songs about their faith. We were afraid of their reaction. But one of the officers came over to me and, with a puzzled look on his face, asked: 'Why are the children singing?' "

A bureaucratic world committed to the exclusion of any purpose except what can be imposed by human will cannot be open to the working of God's Spirit. In such a world, singing seems nonsensical. Yet these children's love overflowed in songs of praise, an activity which the KGB found not so much illegal as unintelligible.

The Book of James contains a passage (5:12-20) that links

the singing of songs with other activities such as praying, suffering, anointing, confessing. The passage seems to suggest that "singing of songs of praise" is a sign of salvation that reflects God's abundant grace and love, and offers the possibility of sustaining people in joy as well as suffering, bodily cheerfulness as well as spiritual pain, eschatological anticipation as well as haunting memories.

Perhaps the KGB officer sensed a threat to the Soviet order in the children's singing, but he did not recognize how transformative singing praise of God can be. Singing together unites, or reunites, people by redrawing the boundaries of community in which there is a responsibility both to perform and to listen—precisely the kind of active receptivity that opens us to God, one another, and a deeper understanding of ourselves.

In his recent book *Self and Salvation,* David Ford explores powerfully the theological significance of singing in community. "Sounds do not have exclusive boundaries—they can blend, harmonize, resonate with each other in endless ways. In singing there can be a filling of space with sound in ways that draw more and more voices to take part, yet with no sense of crowding. It is a performance of abundance, as new voices join in with their own distinctive tones. There is an 'edgeless expansion' (Begbie), an overflow of music, in which participants have their boundaries transformed. The music is both outside and within them, and it creates a new vocal, social space of community in song."

Countless examples in the history of the church and of social movements exemplify how singing has sustained communities and created contexts for transformation. Slaves singing in the rush arbors, choirs singing in medieval cathedrals, people singing "shaped notes" in early American churches, civil rights marchers singing "We Shall Overcome," children singing in Estonian churches.

The Letter to the Ephesians emphasizes the power of

singing, explicitly contrasting singing to drunkenness. Ford's comments on this passage are illuminating: "Singing psalms, hymns and spiritual songs, by contrast [to drunkenness], enables a 'sober intoxication' which attunes the whole self— body, heart and mind—to a life attentive to others and to God. It is a practice of the self as physical as drinking—and as habit-forming. One of the main habits formed is that of alertness. There is also the habit of obedience, a word closely connected in many languages with hearing. Singing is a model of free obedience, of following with others along a way that rings true. In this often the body leads the self, and we find ourselves absorbed in a meaning which only gradually unfolds and pervades other spheres."

Often the body leads the self. One of the reasons that music is so powerful in shaping community, in sustaining people amid oppression or grief, in causing us to overflow in praise, is that singing engages our body and passions as well as our mind, forming us to desire the right things rightly. Singing calls us out of the immediacy of our current situation into a world far greater than we could otherwise imagine.

Perhaps that is why I found myself so moved by the singing of the "Hallelujah Chorus" as the benediction of my father's memorial service. I was really in no mood to hear it, even sung by an assembled choir of friends and strangers. I was grieving, and I felt isolated from God and others. Even so, as the choir sang, I found my body straightening. I eventually discovered that I was on tiptoes. Later a friend told me I had begun singing with the choir. I was drawn out of my grief and isolation, called back into relation with God and the community, in spite of myself.

"Why are they singing?" the KGB officer asked. Because even good habits are hard to break. Once caught by the sober intoxication of singing, of forming and re-forming communities through song, it is very difficult to get people to stop. Oppressors can take away physical freedom or material goods, but they can't take away people's music. In the midst of Nazi Germany, a guard commented that the disruptive singing led by a priest came not only from people but seemed to be "in the bricks."

Why are they singing? Because their lives overflow in God's praise, and because they protest any forms of life where rigid boundaries and false order preclude the edgeless expansion of communal living.

September 8–15, 1999

Reflection / Discussion Questions

1. In what ways have you experienced the musical abundance described by David Ford, whether by singing in a choir, by playing an instrument, by listening, or otherwise?

2. St. Augustine said, "He who sings prays twice." What do you think he meant by this? What role does singing play in the worship life of your congregation?

3. Read the similar verses in Ephesians 5 and Colossians 3 that encourage the singing of psalms, hymns, and spiritual songs. What connection does there seem to be between such musical worship and the life of holiness that is also described in the same passages?

4. Read the story of Paul and Silas in prison in Acts 16:16-40. Why do you think they were singing that night in prison? What does their singing tell you about their character?

43

CHAIN OF HOPE

DURING THE YEARS of apartheid in South Africa, most of the Methodist Church's involvement in education was halted by the government. Schools were closed, land was confiscated and obstacles to new efforts were set in place.

The apartheid government seemed to know just what a threat church-sponsored educational institutions could be. After all, Nelson Mandela was educated at Methodist institutions. Robert Sobukwe, the founder of the Pan-Africanist Congress and the architect of the protests that led to the Sharpeville massacre in 1960, was educated at Methodist schools and was a Methodist lay preacher.

This summer, as my wife and I traveled through the new South Africa, we sensed the pain of Methodists as they talked about the struggles to reassert their commitment to education. We were taken to a beautiful place just outside Pretoria where the Methodists are establishing a theological college on a portion of land that once housed a much larger college. Now businesses, houses and even a police complex exist on what was formerly the church's land for education.

This tragic history has significantly weakened the Methodist Church's ability to provide much-needed education for South Africans as they seek a future unbound by the destructiveness of the past.

The Methodist Church does not have the finances or

infrastructure to fully reestablish its engagement in higher education overnight, but it has taken bold and creative steps. Over the past several years, the church has started more than 60 preschools in churches in the Johannesburg area. The Methodists refer to this project as "a chain of hope."

Education is a commitment to hope for the future at any age. Clearly, preschools offer a sign of hope for the long-term future, even if they don't offer some of the most immediately needed training for rebuilding a nation. And they are a good place to start, if for no other reason than that it is far less expensive to establish preschools in churches than to find the land, the money and the infrastructure to establish high schools, colleges or seminaries.

There are other reasons. In many settings the preschools allow single parents to look for jobs so they can provide their children with resources for a better life. Preschools also offer critically important nourishment, structure and social outlets for children who might otherwise experience the hopelessness that pervades communities racked by poverty, crime and AIDS.

My wife and I could feel the hopefulness in the preschools we visited. This was true wherever we went—whether in the large, multiethnic setting of downtown Johannesburg or in the impoverished township of Ivory Park where the people start a new preschool every time they begin a new congregation. We were moved by the vitality among the teachers, the excitement and warmth among the children. Children have such resilience and optimism that we couldn't help sensing their happiness and the possibilities for their future.

But if this commitment were dependent on childlike optimism, or even on our tendencies to sentimentalize the innocence of children, there would be little reason for hope. After all, one could not help noticing the bars on the windows of some of the schools, or the shacks in Ivory Park where children and their families live. Can these schools educate children in ways that at least acknowledge the larger pain, suffering and struggles in South Africa?

They are trying. In many congregations, preschools are part of larger visions of ministry that include programs designed to foster reconciliation, the healing of memories and economic development. The Methodist Church has developed curriculum for the "chain of hope" preschools that, in age-appropriate ways, helps children begin to acknowledge the importance of healing memories. The church is aware that even young children have been scarred by the past, and live in families and communities where that pain and suffering is palpable. Often the resilience and optimism of children can mask the wounds that, left untreated, make it increasingly difficult for those children to discover and renew hope as they grow toward adulthood.

Could it be that there is nothing as important for the future as the ways in which we educate and care for the youngest children—their souls as well as their minds and bodies? Do we tend to underestimate what children are capable of understanding, of needing, of experiencing?

While in South Africa, I was reading Toi Derricote's powerful memoir, *The Black Notebooks: An Interior Journey*, a tale of growing up black in America. Derricote reflects on an elementary-age black child for whom hopelessness has already set in: "How did this happen? By first grade it is already too late, and in spite of her mother, who spent her maid's paycheck on a white pinafore so that Clarissa would fit in, she *doesn't* fit in, and her mother isn't strong enough to beat that devil out of her."

By first grade, it is already too late. Perhaps unshackling the chains of suffering and creating chains of hope will take longer and will be more difficult than we would like to think. But that work is a sign of authentic hope. After all, we follow someone who said, "Let the children come unto me; do not stop them; for it is to such as these that the kingdom of God belongs."

October 18, 2000

Reflection / Discussion Questions

1. In your observation, how do church-affiliated preschools or elementary schools affect the life of the congregation and / or the community?
2. How significant a role do you think American churches are playing in the Christian formation of children? Explain your answer. How might we benefit from a commitment to Christian education similar to that shown by the Methodist congregations in South Africa?
3. In Matthew 19:13-15, we find one account of Jesus' generous dealings with children. What do you think it is about children that made them so special in Jesus' ministry? How can you and your congregation value the education and spiritual formation of children in a way that reflects your hope for the future?

44

SOME KIND OF TOMORROW

How CAN HOPE be sustained when traumatic memories of conflict or oppression haunt a person or group? This question has become central in a course I am teaching with an African-American colleague. In "Remembrance and Reconciliation," we are examining the legacies of racism and racial division in South Africa and the U.S. Not surprisingly, our discussions quickly focused on issues of despair and hope. Traumatic events and the remembrance of them can transform optimism into despair and occlude any sense of hope for a different and better future.

Toni Morrison's classic novel *Beloved*, one of the texts we've studied, pointedly addresses such issues and has compelled us to ask whether, in the wake of horrifying suffering and sin, hope can be discovered and sustained as an antidote to despair. Early in the story Paul D and Sethe, both former slaves living in the 1870s in Ohio, are discussing some of their experiences. But they do not get very far.

> Paul D had only begun, what he was telling her was only the beginning when her fingers on his knee, soft and reassuring, stopped him. Just as well. Just as well. Saying more might push them both to a place they couldn't get back from. He would keep the rest where it belonged: in that tobacco tin in his chest where a red heart used to be. Its lid rusted shut.
>
> They both knew that memories of the past might take

them to a place from which they would not return. So Paul D kept them in the only safe space he knew—inside the tobacco tin in his chest that had replaced a beating heart.

Similarly, Sethe's "brain was not interested in the future. Loaded with the past and hungry for more, it left her no room to imagine, let alone plan for, the next day." Indeed, it was never too early for Sethe to start the day's serious work of "beating back the past."

Paul D and Sethe both search for some kind of sanctuary or "safe space" where they can cope with memories and find hope. There are brief moments where they begin to glimpse such a space. But they are unable to stay there; the safe space can't be sustained. Why not?

In part, the problem seems to be that Paul D and Sethe understandably but mistakenly look for some timeless place where there is no threat. They are searching for a way of coping with the overwhelmingly *time-full* memories of the past—but no timeless space exists. Hope can be found only if there is a way to deal with the past. Consequently, the haunting, unresolved memories intrude unless resolution, perhaps even forgiveness, can be discovered.

This problem is made more intense by the recognition that even well-intentioned communities that seek to offer sanctuary may not have the strength to cope with the threat of someone's psychic disintegration. As my colleague asked, "When people reach their breaking point and face the threat of disintegration, can a community keep connected to them? If so, how?"

The novel suggests that many communities will not keep connected because they fear their own disintegration. They will expel, or at least marginalize, those among them who are broken, in order to try to preserve even a fragmented identity and coherence.

Can hope be discovered and sustained for those who have gone beyond their breaking point? It would be trite simply to suggest that the answer lies in Jesus.

Even so, the haunting questions of *Beloved* offer an

opportunity for a faithful Christian response. After all, at the end of the novel, Paul D tells Sethe, "Me and you, we got more yesterday than anybody. We need some kind of tomorrow." Christians believe that through Jesus Christ, God provides all people that "some kind of tomorrow" that makes life today possible.

This tomorrow happens not as an escape from time, but through the incarnate, crucified and risen Christ who breaks into time and redeems it. We will not find authentic hope, much less sustain it, by trying to flee time, but only by finding the resources to bear, and bear witness to, the past.

Where can we find those resources? How can we cultivate Christian communities capable of bearing authentic witness to Christ, of sustaining hope even for those who are haunted by memories? A first step is to recognize that such communities are fundamentally time-full, and need to be attentive to their own fragility. Communities as well as individuals can reach their breaking points, and communities as well as individuals can end up holding tobacco tins with lids rusted shut in those places where a red heart used to be.

Might we find those resources in the timeful practices and friendships of communities that know their vulnerability because they are marked as the body of (the crucified and risen) Christ? In communities that gather not to provide illusory "order" but rather to be re-membered by the audacious grace and forgiveness of God in Christ?

We'll find what we need in communities that gather to remember that *all* of us have had too much yesterday, and thus need redemption to sustain us in hope, and in communities that rediscover hope each day in prayer. These communities represent not timeless spaces, but redemptive relationships in which people refuse to abandon those who have suffered and are suffering. These communities offer a tomorrow.

March 7, 2001

Reflection / Discussion Questions

1. What kind of yesterdays would you say you have had? Are there yesterdays that cause you pain and that you would like to have forgiven and redeemed?
2. Do you think people with sordid and difficult yesterdays that are not well hidden are welcomed in your congregation? What can your congregation do to become a place that offers Christ's tomorrow?
3. Jeremiah 29:11 is a favorite passage for many Christians. Read this promise given to the Judahites who faced the desolation of exile, and reflect on / discuss the faithfulness of God to give us also a hope and a future.
4. The power of sin plagues our yesterdays, but Jesus has secured for us a hopeful future. Do you have Christian friends who can walk with you in the processes of repentance and forgiveness as you follow Christ into a new tomorrow? Reflect on / discuss what a new tomorrow would look like, and give thanks to God for the hope we have in Jesus Christ.